PRAY &
PROTECT

PRAY &
PROTECT

PRACTICAL WAYS TO KEEP YOUR CHURCHES AND MINISTRIES SAFE

Dr Patrick Sookhdeo

PRAY & PROTECT
PRACTICAL WAYS TO KEEP YOUR CHURCHES AND MINISTRIES SAFE

Second edition, January 2017

Copyright © Patrick Sookhdeo, 2017

Library of Congress Control Number: 2017930066

ISBN: 978-0-9977033-2-0

Published in the United States by
Isaac Publishing, 6729 Curran Street, McLean, VA 22101

First published in the United States, February 2016

Printed in the United States

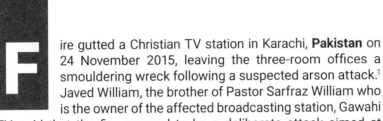

ire gutted a Christian TV station in Karachi, **Pakistan** on 24 November 2015, leaving the three-room offices a smouldering wreck following a suspected arson attack.[1] Javed William, the brother of Pastor Sarfraz William who is the owner of the affected broadcasting station, Gawahi TV, said that the fire seemed to be a deliberate attack aimed at thwarting the Christian work of the station, *"This is not an attack on us; it is an attack on Christianity. Whoever did this does not want God's work to happen."*

Explosives were thrown into the stove chimney of a Kazakh house church in **Mongolia** on the night of 27 December 2015, just days after the local church had celebrated Christmas.[2] *"Believers decided not to come together for a while,"* he said, *"they [are] afraid of a repetition of the explosions in the homes of believers."*

In early 2016, the Evangelical Fellowship of **India** published a report[3] of persecution against Christians during 2015. Physical violence, including assaults by mobs, beatings and torture, were the most common with 68 cases, followed by stopping of worship in churches (18 cases) and attacks on churches (18 cases). Arrests of pastors and their companions was a major issue with 18 cases. At least three cases of rape were recorded.

Suicide bombers, thought to have been commissioned by Boko Haram,[4] blew themselves up in a marketplace at around noon on 27 January 2016 in the mainly Christian town of Chibok, **Nigeria**, where 274 girls were kidnapped by jihadists in April 2014. They then attacked again two days later in the predominantly Christian town of Gombi, in Adamawa state.

1 https://barnabasfund.org/news/Pakistani-Christian-TV-station-reduced-to-rubble-and-ashes-after-suspected-arson-attack [viewed 14/4/2016]

2 https://barnabasfund.org/news/Christians-in-Mongolia-afraid-after-Kazakh-house-church-attack [viewed 14/4/2016]

3 https://barnabasfund.org/news/New-report-reveals-catalogue-of-abuse-against-Christians-in-India-during-2015 [viewed 14/4/2016]

4 https://barnabasfund.org/news/Christian-towns-targeted-in-suicide-bomb-attacks [viewed 14/4/2016]

CONTENTS

CHAPTER ONE
INTRODUCTION

This book is designed to assist ministry leaders in contexts of persecution as they consider the risks and challenges they face from those who are hostile to the Lord's work.

Good ministry leadership will normally already have thought about a number of risks and have in place policies and procedures to reduce dangers and deal with any problems that might arise. These measures are wise and are taken for the care of the church, ministry staff or those people you are caring for.

This booklet aims to build on the good practice of your organisation, but focuses on one specific aspect of care and protection: security measures in contexts of persecution and guarding against attack from people who are hostile to Christianity. It should be emphasised that this issue should not be approached with fear or a spirit of hostility to any enemies, but firstly with prayer and then with a response of Christ-like love. Many of those of other faiths, and of no faith, are not violent, even verbally. In many contexts the risk is low for physical attack, arrest, legal problems or any other measures that could be taken against you.

However, the risk is not zero, and prudence would suggest that a clear-headed analysis is needed to evaluate the level of risk and what reasonable precautions should be taken. The risk of major fire is low, but it does happen somewhere each day and you probably have fire extinguishers in your building in case it happens to you.

This booklet will help you become more aware of the issues and your own environment, will assist in assessing risk, and will provide some useful lines of thought and action. The goal is to implement sensible steps to reduce risk and the impact of any incident that might happen. And if you should suffer a tragic incident, these preparations will help you look after the victims and rebuild.

It is clear that there are many different contexts of persecution around the world, and some sections of this book may be more relevant than others in certain countries. Feel free to use the sections that are most useful to you in your context, but do scan the whole book to see all the areas addressed.

We would welcome questions and feedback.

info@barnabasfund.org

The Pew Research Centre, in their report of 26 February 2015,[1] highlighted the fact that 27% of all countries in the world have high levels of social hostility to religion and a similar percentage of countries where there are high levels of official restriction on religion. Globally, approximately 40% of countries have high levels of hostility or restrictions on religion, often against Christianity.

It is estimated that about 200 million Christians live in countries where there is a significant level of anti-Christian persecution, discrimination or disadvantage. So if you live or operate a ministry in a country where you are at risk, because you are a Christian or work in Christian ministry, then you are not in an unusual position. Christians are the religious group that is globally persecuted the most, in over 100 countries. Christians can be persecuted by people of other religions or ideologies, or by dictatorial regimes, and can find that whole societies or powerful groups within society are hostile in a wide variety of contexts.

Barnabas Fund identifies two general sources of persecution: *top-down* and *bottom up*. In many countries both occur. *Top down* persecution comes from the government, officials, police, the legal system and dominant religious or political groups. *Bottom up* persecution comes from society at large, from family, community, school, work colleagues and hostile unofficial groups.

---

1 http://www.pewforum.org/files/2015/02/Restrictions2015_fullReport.pdf [viewed 15/8/2016]

In many contexts, the attitudes of government, officials and police reflect popular hostility to Christianity by the majority population. Politicians may amplify anti-Christian rhetoric as a way of gathering popular support, especially at election time or when they are under pressure. Competing politicians may try to be more anti-Christian than their rivals, in order to prove that they are more righteous within the majority faith. Militantly anti-religious regimes, such as in China, Vietnam, North Korea or Laos, will have their own ideological motives for persecuting Christians.

The situation can be more difficult if political parties are overtly religious, such as the Bharatiya Janata Party (BJP) in India, or the Muslim Brotherhood in Egypt and elsewhere in the Middle East. If these groups come to power then the state can become very biased against minority groups, and discrimination can be enshrined in the constitution, laws, regulations and policies. In any state where sharia has a major influence or dominant position in the legal system, Christians and other non-Muslim minorities will suffer from a second-class status.

Each church or ministry is different and will have a different approach to dealing with these issues. However, some core requirements are likely to be:

- Direction from the governing body of the ministry e.g. council, trustees, eldership
- Ongoing support from the governing body to the staff
- A small strategic core planning team
- Active involvement of the leadership and staff
- Clear allocation of responsibilities for various parts of your plan
- A timetable for research and implementing your plan
- Regular review of your planning e.g. at least once per year

There may be five areas that you want to consider when planning for risk assessment and measures to protect a church or ministry. These are:

- **Prevention**, for the purposes of this guide, means the measures taken and capabilities necessary to avoid attention or minimise the risk of an attack or incident. Prevention is the action you can take to prevent a potential incident from occurring.
- **Protection** means the policies and capabilities to strengthen churches and ministries against acts of persecution and other threats that might happen. Protection focuses on ongoing actions that protect people, networks, and property from a threat or hazard.
- **Mitigation** means the reduction of the impact of an incident and measures/capabilities necessary to achieve this; reducing loss of life, injury or property damage by lessening the impact of an incident.
- **Response** means the reaction to an incident once it has already happened and capabilities necessary to stabilise the situation, to deal with the incident, save lives and property, help the injured, support those impacted and facilitate the transition to recovery.
- **Recovery** means the process whereby churches or ministries affected by an incident restore their environment and resume normal operations.

Some advice on writing your documents, and planning and communicating with your staff and members:

- Use clear and simple writing in plain language. Summarise important information with checklists and visual aids such as maps and flowcharts.
- Avoid using jargon and minimise the use of abbreviations.
- Use a logical, consistent structure that makes it easy for readers to understand the rationale for the sequence of information and to find the information they need.
- Keep your documents as short as you can, while carrying enough detail.
- Organise the contents in a way that helps users quickly identify solutions and options.

Security measures must be proportional and consistent with Christian values and respect for the rule of law.

CHAPTER TWO
THE GLOBAL ENVIRONMENT

The possibility of a deliberate attack on a church or ministry in your district might have seemed fairly improbable a few years ago.

The rise in religiously motivated violence, even terrorism, with a higher likelihood of serious injury, death or major damage, is a recent phenomenon – even though it was not entirely absent in the past. This can mainly be attributed to events elsewhere in the world, increasing intolerance and developments especially within Islam, nationalist Buddhism and Hinduism.

The resurgence of Islamism or political Islam has seen Islamist violence increase massively over the last two or three decades, mainly in parts of Africa, the Middle East and Asia, but also in Europe and the Americas. Militant strains of Hinduism and Buddhism have also emerged. Nigeria, Central African Republic, Kenya, Syria, Iraq, Pakistan, India, Sri Lanka, Indonesia and Burma (now Myanmar), for example, have seen many incidents of anti-Christian violence in the years since 2000. Dictatorial regimes continue to impose harsh sanctions on groups of which they disapprove in countries like North Korea, China and Vietnam.

Most people in any society will ignore incitement to violence, but a few will be recruited and induced to act. Popular excitement can be generated by an incident, even when the incident is completely fictitious (such as a false blasphemy accusation). Other people may act on their own initiative, small groups of radicals intent on pursuing a particular anti-Christian agenda. Others may be 'lone wolf' individuals who are perhaps copying others.

One of the most dangerous sources of attack can be converts to radical Islam, Buddhism or Hinduism from a nominal community. Converts can often be more fanatical than others, as they seek to prove themselves. They may be motivated to seek the paradise they are promised via a dramatic and violent act.

The risk of attack on Christians appears to increase dramatically when there is a major international crisis that impacts the majority group in your situation. Most obvious here are events that increase agitation among Muslims, for example the *Charlie Hebdo* massacre in Paris in 2015 and the international solidarity messages. The Danish cartoons, the publication of Salman Rushdie's *Satanic Verses* book, or events in the Middle

East are other notable examples. Thus awareness of global international news and the opinions of local Muslims, Hindus, Buddhists, atheists or others will be vital to warn you in advance of increasing tensions. An awareness of active violent groups in your region is also important.

Barnabas Fund analysed[2] a sample selection of 600 attacks on churches in the period 2013–2015. This sample showed attacks occurring in 20 countries. Boko Haram attacked in around 40% of cases sampled, in Nigeria and neighbouring countries like Cameroon. Islamic State and similar groups were involved in attacks in Iraq and Syria. The Niger attacks were triggered by events in Europe related to the *Charlie Hebdo* massacre in Paris and the subsequent publication of cartoons depicting Muhammad. Egyptian attacks were linked to the Muslim Brotherhood and politics in the country. Attacks in Mali were part of Islamist violence in the north of the country. Elsewhere attacks came from the authorities (China, Vietnam), Buddhist nationalists (Burma, Sri Lanka) or Hindu radicals (India).

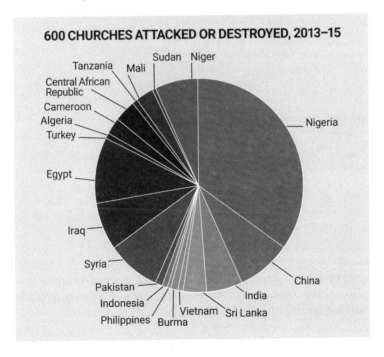

600 CHURCHES ATTACKED OR DESTROYED, 2013–15

---

2 "Persecution in Practice", Barnabas Aid September/October 2015

Another Barnabas study in the same publication looked at deadly incidents and counted casualties, dead and injured, by terrorist group.

Boko Haram, Islamic State and associates, Taliban and al-Shabaab, are the four terrorist groups who are currently the most dangerous for Christians. The chart also shows in which countries the main terrorist groups have killed Christians.

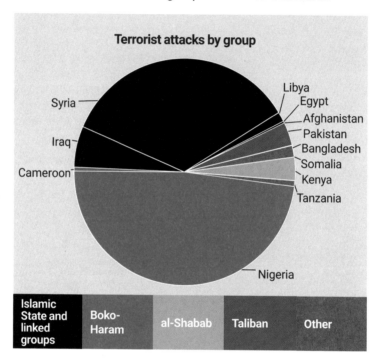

While all four groups have influence right across the more violent Islamist tendencies, it should be noted that Boko Haram originated in Nigeria and has an impact in neighbouring countries, Islamic State originated in Syria-Iraq and has offshoots and supporters particularly in Arabic-speaking regions, the Taliban is rooted in Afghanistan and has affiliations in Pakistan, and al-Shabaab originated in Somalia and links most easily with Somalis and other East African Muslims.

CHAPTER THREE
THE LOCAL ENVIRONMENT

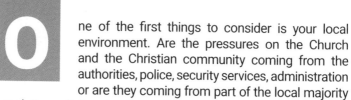

ne of the first things to consider is your local environment. Are the pressures on the Church and the Christian community coming from the authorities, police, security services, administration or are they coming from part of the local majority population, religious leaders, militant groups, terrorists? Are there specifics to your country, perhaps due to history or culture or other influences that make some threats more likely than others?

One very important factor will be the attitude of the legal system, police, authorities and other official bodies. What is the place of Christians/churches in the constitution, the legal system, the administrative rules and regulations? In some countries it is difficult to form a Christian church or association, and very hard to register officially. In such situations, it is very hard to operate legally, if the law says that to gather for worship, prayer, ministry or other 'religious activities' you much belong to a registered group and meet in a registered building.

Your response to such restrictions may depend on a number of factors, including: how strictly enforced the rules are; how harsh the authorities are; and what you think is the right attitude in the face of this type of persecution. In some countries (e.g. North Korea, Afghanistan, Iran, Mauritania) Christians operate in secret "underground churches", hiding carefully from the authorities and their neighbours, very much like the Early Church under Roman persecution.

In other countries Christians try to obey the administrative rules but in the meantime continue to gather without authorisation. In some cases Christian groups challenge rules and regulations that may actually themselves be illegal under the country's constitution and commitments to human rights conventions. This area is more fully covered under the section on human rights and advocacy (Chapter 10).

There may be a large spectrum of situations even within one country. If your group, church or ministry is based in a more cosmopolitan urban environment, such as the capital city, it may be much safer than if it were based in a conservative rural district with much more traditional attitudes.

It makes good sense to understand something about the status and make-up of the local population where you are. What is the ethnic/religious demography? Are there any other minority groups? Is the majority hostile to Christianity? Is this hostility latent or active? What is the political make-up of the local government? Is it modern/secular in outlook with a strong view on the rule of law, peace, justice for all and stability. Or is it influenced by local religious or political groups who are hostile to Christianity?

You may find that other groups, churches or ministries have already considered all these issues and have had security plans in place for many years. If your group, church or ministry is not engaged with a larger association, denomination or other Christian group in some way, is this something you would want to address?

In assessing a terrorist risk from militant Islamists, Hindus, Buddhists or other groups, you should consider what affiliation local mosques, temples and other religious centres have and what is the attitude of local groups? There is, for example, a wide spectrum within Islam, with major differences in doctrine and practice, and major differences in association with terrorist violence. You may find that the local imam and other Muslim community leaders are actively engaged in combatting extremist ideology.

Are there any local communities or groups particularly impacted by events elsewhere in the world? During the long civil war in Sri Lanka, Tamil communities around the world were very concerned about events in that country and the conflict with the Sinhalese majority.

During times of tension, even war, between Pakistan and India, relationships were often strained in the UK between communities with Pakistani/Muslim origins and Indian/Hindu backgrounds. We have seen in recent times that conflict between Sunni and Shia Muslims in the Middle East can have an impact on relations within other countries.[3]

---

3 http://www.yorkshirestandard.co.uk/news/vandals-target-shia-mosque-in-bradford-12642/ and http://www.bbc.co.uk/news/uk-31691120 [viewed 15/1/2016]

For more general considerations, you may want to examine the geographical profile of your district, the needs, tensions and facilities operating within the community. Is it for example a high-crime area, perhaps more unsafe at night, or is it fairly safe at all times? Where are the buildings located that you use, and where do your activities take place, and at what time of the day? Do people have to walk through unsafe areas at night, for example? Do the police patrol the area well?

Where do your leaders and other staff live, and how do they travel and at what times of the day? Are your leaders well known in the community, and are they known for outspoken stances on issues to which some might be hostile? Is your group active in outreach to others, especially to other faiths that are hostile to Christian evangelism or converts from their own faith? Is your group active in community or social work that other groups may disapprove of, for example women's support groups, safe houses or legal aid to women victims of abuse?

How open are your activities to the general public? Worship services and other events/activities will be open to the public, although you may have stewards and ushers on duty who provide a degree of basic security. But how open or indeed publicised are convert care groups, meetings of the outreach team, the schedule of pastors' meetings, conferences etc?

For all the above local considerations, the key question is: what reactions have they evoked among the local community, or groups within the local community? In a safer country, it is possible that all your leaders and activities are well publicised and open, because you want them known so that people can access them. It is possible that you cannot identify anyone who is likely to be hostile to them. This could be a fairly common situation. However, you may consider that one or two activities could be unpopular with certain groups locally, and that a degree of care is needed to minimise risk.

These considerations are covered in greater detail in the next chapter, looking at risk analysis.

You may want to categorise security situations under perhaps four categories. This will give a better idea about the dangers of the current context, and changes to levels of danger.

Categorisation of Security Levels

- The following classification could be used for a simple visualisation of danger levels. It is intended to help you easily but comprehensively gauge a security environment.
- This classification is based on the perception of the security/ danger situation and does not and cannot factor in or analyse unforeseeable events that could suddenly impact a security environment.
- This classification of security levels focuses on two key elements:

  (a) An analysis of the security environment in which individuals and the Christian community live, and

  (b) A violent or potentially violent activity as a result of the degradation of the security environment.

- The factors identified that determine how secure the environment is include:

  (c) The existence, nature and strength of relationships between communities,

  (d) The presence/absence of antagonistic groups in the locality,

  (e) The strength of one law for everyone and law enforcement by police, and

  (f) The level of impunity of officials within the system.

- Each colour category (green, yellow, orange and red) in the classification shows the features of that security/danger level and the expected response of individuals living in that context.

Level	Green	Yellow
Category	MINIMAL DANGER	LOW LEVEL OF DANGER
Features of the Context	Presence of positive networks, relationships and organisations that foster greater well-being among communities Absence of antagonistic groups seeking to cause harm to a particular community Existence of law and government policies that are transparent, built on consensus and strongly enforced Level of impunity is very low. Government officials generally work diligently towards the betterment of the country and with strong checks and balances in the system	Presence of both positive and negative networks and relationships Relationships between communities are somewhat uncertain Antagonistic groups may be present but they are marginal and their activity is neither consistent nor significant Government policies are made mostly transparent and policies are mainly neutral Level of impunity of government officials is low but there can be official bias against Christians. Enforcement of law and policies is reasonable but not as strong as it should be
Expected Response	You live in a safe and secure environment where violence is a rarity Daily life is usually free of extra-ordinary events However, it is important to be watchful since unexpected events may occur	There is no need to be very worried. Situations of violent persecution will occur only rarely, but it is still very important to be prepared for events if they do Daily life continues as usual

Orange	Red
DANGER IS VISIBLE AND LOW-LEVEL HOSTILITY IS PRESENT	**HIGH LEVELS OF DANGER IN A TENSE ENVIRONMENT**
Presence of significant negative relationships in the midst of a few positive relationships in community networks and relationships	Relationships between different groups and communities are confrontational, tense and prone to violence
Strong presence and influence of antagonistic groups in the public space	Clear and present danger from antagonistic groups operating in the environment
Government policies are not neutral and often biased against Christians	The law is not equal for all
Level of impunity for government officials for persecution is high	Government policies may be biased
Low-level hostile activity that is mostly easily contained – protests, isolated incidents, media bias	Officials, police and others are hostile rather than neutral
Presence of hostile radical groups in the locality	Nature of persecution is well organised, targeted and frequent
Occasional violent incidents	Level of impunity is very high
	Frequent (moderate to high intensity) activity
Individuals living in this context have to constantly watch their back for fear of sudden harm. Daily life can continue but Christians operate with some caution	The security environment for Christians is poor, leading to targeted and organised violence
	Be constantly on guard because a situation of great danger may arise without warning. Daily life can continue but Christians operate with great caution

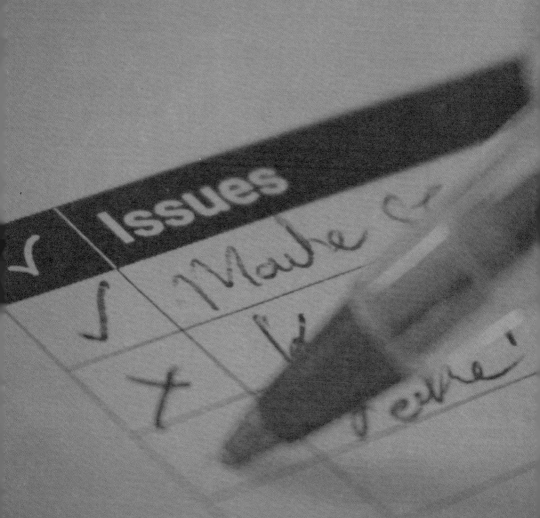

CHAPTER FOUR
RISK ANALYSIS

argets for persecution are often selected for their symbolic value or for a particular reason. Church buildings are visible symbols of Christianity. Targeting religious symbols could also be seen as a way of striking back against 'Western' policies and actions, when people erroneously think that the West is Christian. High-profile leaders could be targeted for their status. Other leaders and staff might be targeted because of the nature of their work. Converts from other religions are often highly vulnerable. Some targets may just be chosen as part the struggle of Islam/ Hinduism /Buddhism/Communism against Christianity and the hoped-for eventual absolute dominance of the local majority.

From the previous chapter you may have a better idea of where the threat may come from, how it may manifest itself, and what the targets might be. The State may have a general policy of hostility to Christianity. Communist regimes have traditionally persecuted Christians quite harshly, as they view allegiance to any other Higher Authority independent from the Party/State as treasonable. Many dictatorial regimes have a similar attitude. Persecution will be difficult to avoid, as a strong State has a wide range of measures it can take: judicial or extra-judicial killing, arrest and imprisonment of pastors, closure of churches and other organisations, arrest and imprisonment of church members, fines, regulatory restrictions, confiscation of Bibles and other materials, and police brutality. The State also often has control over much of the media, and so there will often be campaigns of false information to the general population.

The local majority population may be traditionally hostile, or encouraged to new hostility by militant religious and political leaders. In India, for example, the situation has become much more difficult for Christians since the coming to power in 2014 of President Modi and the militant BJP Hindu party. Here there is a dangerous mixture of political authority with local BJP party leaders and local mob violence. In Muslim contexts there can be similar combinations of radical political leaders, religious leaders and popular prejudice against non-Muslim minorities. Pakistan is an example of this, where some political leaders seeking the votes of the militant Islamist section of majority society, combine with radical Islamist clerics, and facilitate the prejudices of mob violence.

Sometimes the threat may come from small radical groups who are anti-Christian, even if they are also hostile to the State and not supported by many in the majority community. In such cases the risk may come in the form of terrorist attacks.

Terrorists or attacks with a terrorist element seek to generate public shock and fear, and an attack on a church building or Christian leadership would have high public visibility. The aim may also be to eliminate Christian leaders, or Christian centres of activity. If the enemies of Christianity can close down a centre or a ministry, they will feel that they are advancing their goals.

Churches could be targeted to create social tensions and widen divisions. Jihadi doctrine includes the strategy provoking divisions, harsh security measures and official reactions that may draw other Muslims towards radicalisation and recruitment into their ranks. Remember that Salafists are strongly opposed to any liberal or moderate trends within Islam, and want to radicalise the Muslim community. Much the same is the case with militant Hindus or Buddhists. In some cases groups or individuals want to prove that they are effective in opposition to Christianity, and so show that they are 'better' among other members of their religion or tendency.

A potential church attacker may not come from a coherent group, and could be a lone individual, perhaps someone psychologically troubled. They could be a recent convert to their faith or a particular branch of its ideology, imbued with an indiscriminate enthusiasm for the more radical expressions of their new faith. Nevertheless 'lone-wolf' attackers are likely to have been influenced by extremist ideology, and so in some ways the background thinking to any terror plot would be similar.

Risk is likely to be higher when there are high-profile events somewhere in the country that raise the level of anger or resentment within a local community. For example, in some Muslim communities, the following typical issues could ignite local passion about events elsewhere:

- Political elections, where there is an Islamist agenda
- Political campaigns inducing tension e.g. drives to establish more sharia in a country or district
- Debate over religious laws, and the possibility of changes
- Accusations of Christians blaspheming or desecrating Qurans, even if such accusations are false or flimsy
- Military operations against Islamist groups or rebels
- Christian mission work especially if celebrating large numbers of conversions from Islam to Christianity
- Fatwas (Islamic legal opinions) calling for attacks on pastors, missionaries and churches
- Media reports or public discussion of human rights issues; criticism of high-profile apostasy cases, blasphemy cases, inhumane Islamic punishments or similar
- Criticism of Islam generally or any revered Muslim figures (Muhammad particularly)
- During the Islamic month of Ramadan, jihadi leaders often call for heightened terror activities during this 'holy' period

Making a risk assessment

A risk assessment looks at three things; the type of risk, the likelihood of the event happening, and the impact if it does happen. Some possibilities are very unlikely, but they could have a large impact so need to be considered. Other possibilities are highly likely, but have a small impact, so the measures you take are fairly straightforward and minimal. The most important risks are those that are moderately likely and/or could have a big impact.

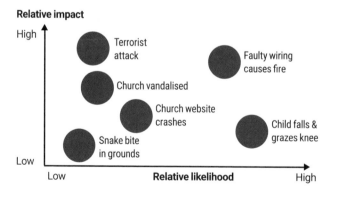

Relative impact

High

Terrorist attack

Faulty wiring causes fire

Church vandalised

Church website crashes

Snake bite in grounds

Child falls & grazes knee

Low

Low   **Relative likelihood**   High

Plotting the risks, the likelihood and the potential impact is a useful exercise.

The next step is to produce a comprehensive Risk Chart that catalogues the issues, the level of assessed risk, what the possible impacts could be, and measures initiated to reduce the risk of something happening or reduce the impact if it does happen. This is possibly the most useful exercise for your church fellowship, and should be given serious attention by the leadership as a whole. You may find that it produces a document that also helps focus on other risks, and defensive actions.

You may want to think in terms of (a) people, (b) ministries/ activities and (c) buildings or locations. You need to think about different types of risks that should be assessed under the general headings, who or what are the possible targets, and what could be the impact of an attack.

- The aim is not to change what the Ministry does
- Curtailing the witness of the Ministry would be a defeat
- The aim is to do things better and more safely, as necessary
- The goal is to be *as wise as serpents and as innocent as doves* [Matt 10 v 16]
- There is no such thing as zero risk, nor is zero risk a Biblical approach to ministry and service
- Plans and precautions need to be devised, known and owned by all leadership/staff/volunteers

Example of one page from a hypothetical risk assessment document

ISSUE	RISK LEVEL	IMPACT	COUNTER-ACTIONS
Arson	Medium	Loss of building or parts of it Loss of meeting place Loss of equipment and material Cost of rebuild or repairs Decline in congregation	Appropriate buildings/contents insurance Good physical security Alarms and links to fire brigade Possible counter-measures e.g. sprinklers Plan B for alternative place to meet
Theft of data	High	Breach of Data Protection Act Loss of sensitive data Risk to individuals	Secure storage of data Well-protected systems Care over publication of information
Lone wolf attack on church service	Low	Death or injury	General security measures CCTV Training of ushers/stewards First aiders always available
Attack on a convert	Medium	Death or injury Fear Person leaves the church	Protective measures Group support
Attack on pastor	Low	Death or injury Loss of pastor for a period	General security measures CCTV, intercom on door Working in a team
Suicide bomber	Low	Death or injury Fear Loss of building or parts of it Loss of meeting place Loss of equipment and material Cost of rebuild or repairs Decline in congregation	Security measures including CCTV Good physical security Trained stewards, parking controls Appropriate buildings insurance cover Appropriate contents insurance cover Plan B for alternative place to meet

Where does the threat come from?

- Government and officials, police?
- Local religious or political leaders? Acting with official or mob support?
- The community in general? Acting with official support?
- Elements within the community? Acting with official or mob support?
- Individuals or small groups? Acting with official or public support?
- Terrorist groups?

Ministries and activities

What different ministries and activities does your group operate?

- Church services, prayer and other meetings?
- House or cell groups?
- Evangelism and outreach?
- Convert care and discipleship training?
- Ministries to women?
- Youth activities?
- Social or community activities?
- Church schools or school activities?
- Health programmes?
- Community programmes?
- Activities involving members of other faiths?
- Human rights activities and advocacy?
- Where do they meet?
- When do they meet?
- Who runs them?
- Are they open to the public?
- How well known or publicised are they in the area?

Are any of these activities more likely to be unpopular with any group?

Community projects (perhaps lower risk?)

Convert care programmes (higher risk?)

Four key security questions

There are four key questions to address when thinking about security. They are:

1. Security **of** what: Who or what do you want to protect?
2. Security **from** what: What is the threat or who are the people who may attack you?
3. Security **for** what: What benefit will a security improvement bring to the potential target?
4. Security **by** what: Refers to how you might enhance the security of the potential target?

CHAPTER FIVE
SITE SECURITY

Buildings

Ministry buildings, churches, church schools, kindergartens, church halls, clinics, meeting rooms, hostels, orphanages etc. are visible buildings/activities that are often seen as symbols of Christianity or representative of the faith.

They can be vulnerable targets because they are:

- Easy to access
- Often open to the public
- Routinely visited by strangers
- Largely unprotected
- Static i.e. easily located for attack
- Can be targeted at virtually any time of choice

The structure of a building can have significant impact on the level of risk; does it have a perimeter wall, gates, stone or wooden walls, large windows that could send shards of glass flying if there was an explosion of any type?

Physical security

How well protected and physically secure are the physical sites you use? This is a question to consider in terms of protecting against theft, vandalism, arson and physical attack. Please note that no building can be made 100% sure against agents of the state, or a mob, or terrorist attack, but even here sensible measures can be taken to mitigate the risks.

- Do you own your sites or are they borrowed/rented e.g. a hall?
- Physical aspects of the site: construction material of the building, large amounts of glass in walls/doors/windows (and danger of flying shards), measures you can take to improve resistance to attack?
- Security of the various sites: walls and fences, secure doors, windows and locks?
- Are windows fitted with security bars?
- When are buildings open/locked?
- Are internal offices/rooms locked when unused?
- Do you have a strong fire-proof safe for vital documents and/or money?
- How do you control access to your buildings?
- How well are keys monitored and who has access to them?
- Who is on-site when buildings are open, are they working alone?
- Do you have any alarm systems?
- Do you have adequate escape routes e.g. in case of fire?
- How easily can the alarm be raised? How? With whom?
- How can you help emergency vehicles access the site when needed?

When considering site security it is good to examine security measures from the outside and work inwards, i.e. from the external public areas, looking at perimeter security and then progressively inwards. This would be the point of view of someone planning to attack you.

The aim is to provide several layers of barriers to intruders, making it difficult for them to gain entry to the main building and increasing the chance of early detection. Probably the key line of defence is the shell of each building, and the walls, roof, doors and windows are the main items to consider. Are each of these points solid and reasonably capable of resisting entry by intruders?

How do you control vehicle access to your site? How close to the building can a vehicle approach? With the increase of vehicle bombings / suicide attacks using cars or trucks, many centres are erecting barriers so that vehicles cannot approach the building too closely. This has saved multiple lives in a number of cases.

Surrounding a site with substantial fencing/walls can significantly improve security. It can also act as a deterrent, and as a psychological barrier, by demarcating the site so intruders know they are trespassing. However. walls and fences will not stop a determined attacker and so should not be at the expense of additional measures.

Depending on the use of your site, again it may be important to think about what you are protecting against. Many barriers will stop or at least impede intruders. But if the risk is a drive-by shooting, say someone on a motorbike with a gun, then a fence, hedge or railings will offer much less protection than a solid wall. Likewise a high wall protects against people being easily able to observe what happens inside your compound.

In general, perimeter walls/fencing should be at least 2.4 metres or 8 feet in height to have any real security value against intruders. Be especially careful where a fence joins any other barrier or a different type of fence; it is often at these points that they are easiest to climb.

Where perimeter walls or fencing are erected, adequate gates should also be installed to maintain security levels. Gates should be kept locked outside business hours. A security perimeter is only as strong as its weakest point.

If you are considering the perimeter security, in terms of current strength or because you are thinking about upgrading, the following are likely possibilities:

• PVC/powder-coated weldmesh or expanded metal fencing is difficult to overcome and maintains visibility of an intruder once inside – but can be vulnerable to attack at fixing points to fencing posts

Concrete security barriers for roads and streets

- Timber panels, whilst economical to install, provide a screen for an intruder once scaled and will not present much resistance to physical attack
- Thorn hedging can be used in conjunction with other perimeter protections, has very low maintenance costs and once established acts as an effective deterrent where free from gaps
- Chain-link fencing, readily available, relatively cheap and easy to install, but easier to climb, can distort and is subject to localised collapse following cutting
- Steel palisading is substantial and very effective
- Brick walls are solid barriers and require minimal maintenance. However, they do act as a screen for intruders once they have climbed into the site
- Barbed or razor wire on top of a wall or fence can add significantly to the protection of the site

Active security measures

With the advent of more readily available technology, systems such as CCTV cameras, interphones and security scanners can be added to a site comparatively easily and cheaply. These will be effective against some threats, but may be less useful against others.

It is possible that some measures, such as **CCTV cameras**, may have a range of benefits:

- They act as a *deterrent* to potential attackers, making them unwilling to commit a crime that could be recorded for visual evidence
- CCTV cameras should be positioned in places that are *hard to access*, so making it more difficult for people to disable them
- *Fake CCTV cameras,* that look the same outside but have no working parts, can be mixed with real ones. Place these in more accessible locations, making the fake ones the likely target for any disabling actions and giving the real CCTV cameras a better chance of survival. This provides additional deterrent effect at very low cost
- If an incident does occur, you should have hard film *evidence* to show the police and a better opportunity of gaining justice
- Of course CCTV may not deter a suicide bomber, to take an extreme example, as he/she will not care about being filmed and what might happen after the event e.g. a court case!

Church security team members with scanners

Security paddles or wands act as metal detectors and are commonly used to control access at airports, public buildings and other controlled areas. These are fairly cheap but you need to ensure that you purchase a reliable model, as there are many fairly ineffective items on the market.

Again these will not be effective in all cases of threat but they will allow your stewards to monitor access to a building by checking at the entrance that no one is carrying a concealed weapon or other device. Such equipment, if used, should be part of a comprehensive programme of security, training and back-up for your stewards, ushers, security team etc.

Reception teams, ushers and stewards

Church ushers and stewards, or receptionists in a ministry building, normally have little background in security or protection. However, you may have a police officer, a member of the military, a security worker, or someone retired from one of these fields, known to your fellowship or ministry. Could they help in planning and training?

The role of steward at church or meeting is often thought of as being a friendly greeter, someone to hand out leaflets or song books, and guide people to their seat. Stewards may be expected to pass the collection plate, and have a role during the service or meeting. Fortunately these are likely to continue to be their routine tasks.

However, ushers and stewards are partly responsible for security and safety of the fellowship, along with elders, pastors, deacons and others. Certainly stewards are in the front line in that they are likely to be the first people to have to deal with a visitor, an intruder or a problem outside the building. Stewards may be moderately experienced in dealing with difficult people, perhaps a drunken person who attends a festival or a hostile neighbour who shouts at church attenders.

Stewards and ushers are not expected to act as police officers, and should protect their own safety. However, they should be observant and aware, able to assess situations and respond appropriately. There is a dual role here, of servant to the fellowship/ministry, and guardian. Local police may be able to give you further guidance on the role of stewards.

The role requires a degree of balance: projecting a welcome for visitors yet an awareness of potentially difficult or even dangerous situations. Some stewards are overly relaxed, and engage in a lot of conversation with friends. They may then not be aware of things happening nearby. Others may be extremely anxious, and so tense and on edge a lot of the time and perhaps overly officious.

Signs to look out for in an unknown visitor are various, and there is no easy way to identify a person with problems, a potential aggressor or terrorist. The following signs should cause concern, but be aware that there could also be innocent reasons for any of these behaviours. The first few might be more typical of someone disturbed, or angry with the church/ministry, while the later signs might be more typical of a premeditated attacker/terrorist.

Some tell-tale signs:
- High energy, emotional state
- Muttering, praying, fingering prayer beads
- Sweating heavily in cool weather
- The smell of alcohol
- Loud and boisterous behaviour
- Erratic or aggressive behaviour
- Chest puffing, raised voice or posturing
- Invading the steward's space and using aggressive but not directly harmful physical contact. Poking or shoving can signal the beginning of a confrontation
- The attacker might pick the biggest, strongest steward to confront
- Terrorist attackers often stalk their target until the best opportunity to attack presents itself. Look out for people observing your building for a period before approaching
- If the attackers intend to flee the scene, they may have a suspicious accomplice loitering in a vehicle nearby with the engine running
- An odd heavily laden vehicle
- If you notice an individual who is paying a little too much covert attention to you, or makes you uncomfortable for reasons you can't totally explain, it is often best to share your concerns with others
- Attackers may try to make use of available cover to take their victims by surprise. If you see someone moving in a suspicious way, avoiding places where they can be seen, trying locked entrance doors, attempting to slip round the back of a building, raise your concerns and take action
- Be aware of people carrying bags or other items that could conceal weapons
- Be aware of unattended bags or other containers
- Use caution over unattended bags/containers that could contain a bomb; never try to move or disarm a bomb
- Is the person dressed inappropriately e.g. on a hot day wearing bulky clothing that could be hiding something?

"A gentle answer turns away wrath, but a harsh word stirs up anger."

Proverbs 15 v 1

Stewards must be realistic about a church or ministry environment. People arrive early and late for meetings. People move singly and in groups. People forget things and change their minds. People may roam around the building. The entrance may be packed with people at times. People may be leaving one service/event while others come in for another event. People do strange things, which are perfectly logical to them!

Stewards must be knowledgeable about elements that ought to concern them: the location of emergency exits, evacuation routes and procedures, meeting places, alarms, fire extinguishers and similar. They should be aware of policies and procedures. There should be a senior steward for each event, who will take responsibility, perhaps with a back-up deputy.

Stewards and people with similar roles should be included in any planning about how to deal with an attack on the church or ministry, the elements contained within chapter 12.

Stewards should view themselves as part of a team and ideally should never deal with a dangerous situation alone – always in a two- or three-person group. Always get assistance before approaching someone you are concerned about. You need back-up, and a witness, if anything violent occurs. However, make sure that your group does not project an environment of intimidation or threat – as this could provoke a reaction. A smile and gentle words will often disarm someone hostile.

Evacuation plans

You should have clearly signed evacuation plans and routes, often designed for evacuation in case of fire. You may want to evaluate these in terms of adequacy in case of another type of incident.

- Do you have multiple alternative exit routes?
- Are exit routes kept clear of obstruction and adequately signposted?
- Do you have suitable safe meeting points outside?
- Do you have nominated persons in charge of escape procedures?
- Do you have procedures to quickly call public authorities?
- Do you have trained first aiders available?

CHAPTER SIX
PERSONAL SECURITY

People

Who are the visible leaders and staff in your group, church or ministry? Are any other individuals or groups particularly likely targets or particularly vulnerable? Do you have converts from another faith? Do you have people who are higher profile in the community: lawyers, doctors, political leaders, media spokespeople?

Things to take into account in the risk assessment:

- Where do your leaders, workers and people live/work?
- Who are your higher-profile staff?
- Do key leaders/workers have back-up deputies who can take over if needed?
- How well known or identifiable are individuals in the area?
- When and where do they interact with the public?
- How do they interact with the public?
- Do they have any specific ministries e.g. evangelism, convert care?
- How visible are these ministries and what reaction have they evoked?
- How accessible are they by an attacker?
- Do your staff and other people work alone?
- Who has access to food and food preparation areas?
- How quickly do newcomers have access to sensitive people and areas?
- How quickly do newcomers have access to sensitive information?

Different types of clothing can identify people

Individual security plans

You may need to do some thinking about personal security. This should in any case be a consideration for church or ministry oversight, when taking care of leaders, assistants, other staff and volunteers. You may be able to draw upon security skills/experience within the membership of the local Christian community.

- Working alone is always higher risk
- Individuals alone should always have a mobile phone if possible
- People may need to think about variable travel routes if they are at risk
- It may be advantageous to be or to travel in public spaces with other people around – although this would also make it easier for someone to approach you
- Travelling alone at night is usually a higher risk, especially for women
- Get advice if you are concerned, from the police if they can be trusted
- Should people have some personal security awareness training?

Travel in vehicles

Do you or your team use vehicles in your ministry? Safety on the roads is an important general consideration but you should also consider this from the perspective of an attack on the personnel or work of the church or other organisation.

Vehicles are not all the same; some are stronger, more robust and have better safety features. People often consider cars and other vehicles from the point of view of looks, performance, economy and price. However, you should also consider the use they will have and whether they are well adapted to the road conditions and distances that will be travelled.

However, it is probably more important that a vehicle is looked after, well maintained and operated in an appropriate manner:

- Have the vehicle maintained and repaired by a good garage/mechanic
- Make sure that all legal paperwork is up-to-date and correct
- Regularly check the vehicle for the condition of the tyres, tyre pressure, brakes, steering, oil, brake fluid, radiator, headlamps, tail lights, indicators, windscreen wipers, seat belts etc.
- Visually inspect your vehicle before you get in. If operating in a hostile area, you may want to look under the vehicle too. Dangers can be anything from a nail placed against a tyre to burst it when you start moving, tampering with brakes, or even a bomb under the floor
- Always make sure you have a good margin of fuel for your journey, especially if gas stations will be rare on the route
- Carry spare fuel cans if necessary, but be aware that this needs to be done carefully
- Carry basic items in the vehicle in case of problems: spare tyre, blanket, torch, water bottle, basic vehicle tools. Carry a first aid kit
- Do not overload a vehicle and consider the condition of the roads when loading
- Load a vehicle carefully and ensure that the load is secure. Heavier items should be at the bottom, with lighter items on top. Consider what happens with the load if you have to stop suddenly or have a crash
- Check the weather forecast before starting a major journey, especially if travelling cross-country
- Carry a mobile phone and a charger
- Tell your team your plans, where you are going and when you are traveling
- Do not drive when you are tired and take regular breaks on long journeys, for food and drink
- Travel with someone else if possible, for security, to share the driving and for company
- If travelling in several vehicles, stick together, be clear about what to do if you get separated

CHAPTER SEVEN
FINANCIAL SECURITY

The financial security of your organisation is important and you should take regular steps, perhaps annually, to review the situation. The responsibility for managing and protecting the assets of any church, ministry or NGO rests on the shoulders of the leadership, whether this is a committee, board of trustees, the executive committee, the directors, or the eldership. In many organisations these responsible people may have other roles and see themselves as "just volunteers" for oversight. This chapter will allow you to review your financial security.

An attack on the financial assets of an organisation can be very damaging. This is not just a risk from outside hostile elements but is also an internal risk. There is not just the benefit of damaging your operations but a hostile move on your assets may carry financial benefits to an attacker. Possible scenarios here would include fraud (perhaps by a contractor or an associate), corruption of a member of staff, outright robbery of cash or material goods, theft of PIN codes, hacking into your bank account or accessing credit cards, the introduction of a person who is an 'agent' into your organisation, and possibly official wrong-doing by officials over land or buildings or other assets.

The leadership needs to approach financial affairs from a very business-like perspective. The organisation should have basic policies and procedures in place to protect their financial assets. An organisation should never have the policy of saying: *"We don't worry about financial procedures; we trust our brilliant treasurer to look after the cash!"*

Some people may feel that implementing strict financial controls and security is an insult to the integrity and honesty of their treasurer and others who manage the funds of the organisation. In reality, procedures of this type are as much for the protection of these people as they are for the protection of the organisation. Proper financial procedures help to take the weight off the shoulders of the financial team, improve procedures and accountability, show transparency and reduce opportunities for enemies. A financial scandal is one of the greatest risks to your organisation, as it wrecks your reputation, destroys your resources, drives away members and donors and, perhaps most importantly, is a hugely negative witness to the Gospel.

Signing authority

A standard safeguard in organisations is to require two people to sign all cheques, contracts and financial transactions. In many organisations three or four persons will be authorised to provide the two signatures – so that if one person becomes ill or goes on an extended trip the organisation always has at least two people available to make financial transactions or payments.

This procedure is ineffective if one of the officers signs a quantity of blank cheques in advance. While probably well intentioned, this person has abdicated their duty and has put the organisation's funds at risk. Signing persons and the entire board should always insist on all cheques being fully completed before anyone signs. Officers with signing authority should also want to verify the cheques against the corresponding contracts/invoices/orders before signing.

Regular reporting

The board should specify a regular schedule of financial reporting and the level of detail that they require in those reports. At a minimum, financial reports should indicate the current cash position of the organisation, the inflows and outflows for the reporting period and any outstanding expenses or receipts. Provide copies of the report to all board members. It is the duty of the directors to ensure that they review and understand the financial reports provided.

The financial books or records of the organisation are the property of the organisation and not the treasurer. They should be open for examination at any reasonable time by directors of the organisation.

Annual budgets and spending limits

Spending authority for the signing officers is normally provided in the annual budget of the organisation. In most organisations, the board of directors delegates authority to the signing officers for day-to-day purchases outlined in the budget. This means that the treasurer does not have to wait for approval at a monthly board meeting every time a new pencil needs to be purchased (provided that pencils/office supplies are included in the budget!).

Major expenditure not included in the budget should be approved by motion at a meeting of the board. The executive director may have authority to authorise small items of expenditure, with perhaps a set upper limit.

The organisation may set out spending limits for the officers on major purchases. Expenditures over a predetermined level may require board approval. A sample board policy could state that *"any purchases over $500 require approval by motion at a board meeting"*.

For larger expenditures or for capital expenditures, the organisation should perhaps have a policy that requires a competitive bidding process. Written quotes from two or three potential vendors should be obtained and presented to the board before a purchase is approved, based on the best price/quality.

Cash transactions

Some activities of organisations may be most easily handled with cash. Sometimes this may result in large amounts of cash being handled at one time. Some simple procedures can limit the possibility of theft or any accusations of mishandling cash:

- Have cash receipts counted and recorded as soon as possible from the time that they were received
- Always ensure that there are at least two people present when cash is being handled
- Once cash has been counted, lock it up in a location that can only be accessed by authorised individuals
- Make bank deposits regularly to avoid having significant amounts of cash on the site

In cases where cash is being used, insist on receipts or have the individuals receiving the cash sign a form stating that they have received it.

Cheques

Cheques provide an easy-to-follow paper trail for organisations. However one risk with cheques is the possibility of forgery.

While this risk may appear relatively small, it can be tempting for some individuals to try to pass stolen and forged cheques. The following actions can help reduce this risk:

- Keep all blank cheques in a secure and preferably locked location
- Keep signed cancelled cheques that are returned from the bank in a secure and preferably locked location
- Be careful with incoming cheques. Until the funds have been cleared by your bank, which normally takes several days, the payment has not been made. Never provide goods, services or refunds on cheques that have not been cleared as paid by your bank. The same rules apply for wire transfers that have not been cleared as paid.

Credit and debit cards

Credit and debit cards are convenient and widely accepted and many organisations have decided that it is appropriate for their staff or officers to be issued a card for the organisation. If this is the case, then the officers should meet with officials from their financial institution to discuss the options that can be put in place. These may include daily transaction limits, especially important if the card is lost or stolen. The persons who carry the cards need to have very clear guidelines around the use of these cards. They should also know how to immediately alert the issuing bank if the card is lost or stolen.

Organisation credit cards should never be used for personal expenditure items even if the individual pays their share of the balance as soon as the statement comes due.

Money laundering

Also be cautious of money laundering attempts. "Money laundering" is the process whereby dirty money (proceeds of crime) is "washed" by passing it through several honest transactions, to make it become clean money. This can be done by people paying you money for something and then claiming a repayment at a later date. The dirty money may have come from a criminal source, perhaps robbery, drugs or fraud, but by passing it through the church accounts the money is "cleaned"or "laundered", so that it has a good source when it returns to the criminals. Typical signs of this are: strange or unusual transactions, where people are very anxious to pay you money but most of the money ends up returning to the original payer. There may be a small "profit" for your organisation, but the criminals will regard this as your *fee* for washing the dirty money for them.

Separation of funds

Committees or divisions of an organisation may have separate bank accounts and some may even have their own treasurer. The board of directors of the parent organisation should be aware of these kinds of accounts and authorise the use of them. These accounts should be operated under the same principles as those of the parent organisation, including any requirement for an annual independent financial review.

Committees and divisions of organisations are a part of the larger group. Their money is part of the group's money. They share the responsibilities and accountability. This includes the responsibility to report to the board of directors and the membership an accurate account of the finances. The board will determine the frequency of this reporting, but reports should be presented at least once a year and should be made through the treasurer of the parent organisation.

It is important that an organisation carefully protects funds designed for a specific purpose. If you receive a grant from a donor organisation for a particular project, this money (restricted funds) should not be confused with the general funds of the organisation, even if it is kept within the same bank account. The donor will be very unhappy if in six months' time it is told that the clean water project cannot be achieved because the money has unfortunately been spent on buying a new car for the executive director.

Project reporting

If you receive grants or other donations from outside organisations, perhaps to assist your operations or to finance specific projects, the donor will expect you to supply financial accounts when you report back to them.

It should be remembered that donor organisations will be audited under the rules and regulations in force in their country. Their own supporters will expect good monitoring and reporting on projects to which they have given money. For a good partnership, it is important to be transparent, accurate and prompt in reporting and accounting for project finance. If there are problems, for example cost over-runs on a project, be open in explaining the problem to your partners. A donor would rather know about the issue than have it hidden in fictitious figures. If you have an excess of money remaining after a project, again make this clear while offering to send it back and/or suggesting another local use. Make it a standard rule to send annual audited accounts to major donors.

Independent financial reviews

Every organisation should ideally have their financial affairs examined by an independent, objective and qualified person once a year. A financial review completed by a professional in the field will provide the organisation with a credible opinion about the accuracy of the financial statements, how fairly the statements reflect the financial situation of the organisation and the degree to which the organisation has complied with generally accepted accounting principles. Any concerns about the financial health of the organisation or its financial practices will be brought to the attention of the appropriate people. This type of review provides the board with assurance that the assets of the organisation are being protected and managed properly.

Organisations should review the national legislation under which they are incorporated as well as their own constitution and bylaws for information about the type of financial review required. Organisations that have status as a registered charity may require a higher level of assurance. Granting institutions may also stipulate the level of financial review required before they will agree to provide funding.

The word "audit" is commonly used. An audit is precisely defined by the accounting profession and provides a very high level of assurance for an organisation.

Use of volunteers for financial review

Smaller organisations may find the cost of full accounting services to be very expensive in comparison to their operating budgets. Auditing may not be possible in some contexts, for security reasons. For groups that find themselves questioning the affordability of a professional examination of their financial records there are other options.

You may produce management accounts and just have these signed off by an independent financial person. Some accounting professionals and firms may be willing to provide free or discounted services for not-for-profit groups in their communities. Is this a possibility in your church or community? Take a look at your membership list and see if there are any members who are practicing or retired accounting professionals. These people may be willing to contribute their time and talents from time to time. However, do not use someone who is currently on the board as this can present a conflict-of-interest situation.

As with any volunteer task, it is important to provide the individuals recruited with a clear job description that outlines the tasks to be completed. What records do you want them to examine and in what detail? What type of report is the organisation, and third parties, expecting? When must the task be completed?

Retention of records

Organisations should have policies in place that clearly state the length of time that financial records of the organisation must be kept. This will apply both to physical written records (ledgers, cheques, receipts, etc.) and to electronic records if the treasurer is using a computer programme to manage the finances of the organisation. Seven years is a commonly accepted length of time but choose the length of time that is appropriate for you.

Important or sensitive records should be kept securely, in a safe or in lockable cabinets.

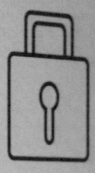

PASSWORD:

****

CHAPTER EIGHT
INFORMATION
SECURITY

hallenges to your data security may well differ in importance, but not in kind, depending on whether you are able to operate openly in your country or whether you are part of an underground church. Data security is always important, but if you are part of a secret group of Christians then it may be a matter of life or death. Likewise if you are working with people under significant threat, for example converts, data security is absolutely vital for them.

You may need to consider what data to record, either electronically or on paper format. Is it necessary to have lists of names and addresses, telephone numbers, personal details? The question needs to be asked: what would happen if this information got into the hands of the authorities or enemies of the ministry? If the information is dangerous, you need to have an overriding reason for keeping it.

Do not neglect to secure paper information as securely as possible, in a safe or in locked filing cabinets. Many organisations are good at protecting electronic data, but leave papers lying around in easily accessible places. Shred or otherwise destroy important papers that you do not need anymore.

One basic way of protecting electronic data is to use a "password protected" Word/Excel document. Under "file" you will find the option of locking the document. Only those people who need to access the document are given the password. The password should not be something too simple, like the name of the organisation, or a person's name, or ABCD1234! It should be at least eight characters long, and include letters, numbers and symbols. If the computer is stolen then the document can only be opened by someone who has the password. Be careful not to forget the password, but do not write it down anywhere that can be easily found! If you have to have a list of passwords, one safer place to keep them is in a password-protected document.

Is it possible to record and retain the actual data in a coded way? Common systems include the use of nicknames rather than real names, simple coding routines for numbers e.g. the 4th and 6th figure of a telephone number are random additions and are ignored when dialling, key places and items have code names.

These will probably be simple systems and codes, easily broken by serious professional work (e.g. by the police) but they may be sufficient to cause thieves and hostile elements some problems.

Even if you are able to operate openly, how well protected is your data; website, emails, computers, electronic documents, membership rolls, names and addresses, telephone numbers, information about individuals?

There are two major risks to consider with data: seizure/theft and loss. Sensitive data that is seized by the authorities or stolen could be used to physically attack the church or attack people, cause arrests or other problems e.g. the pastor or a convert, cause public embarrassment or cause any other nuisance. A takeover and corruption of your website, by a hostile hacker for example, will be a public embarrassment if not worse.

Data that is lost e.g. by fire, virus attack, destruction of systems or corruption of your website, will cause a variety of internal problems for your ministries and administration. However, if the data has not gone out of the organisation then at least it minimises the risk of other problems. So check that data is regularly backed up and secured safely e.g. in a fire-proof metal safe.

Need to know

In more sensitive situations, it may be wise to follow the well-known security motto of only giving information on a "need-to-know" basis. This means information is not generally shared, but only given to people (a) who need to have it and (b) when they need to know it and not before. This requires wisdom from the people with the information, and also from everyone else not to seek to gain more information than they need. The more people who know something, the greater the risk that this information will become public, through accident, gossip, mistake or error.

One obvious aspect of this would be the passwords to your computer systems. Each person should have their own password which they must keep secret. Your computer administrator will have a master password but not know individuals' own passwords. Larger computer systems should register people logging on and logging off the system so as to be able to see who accessing what information, and when. This can be particularly important if someone comes in during the night, logs on, and tries to access or copy sensitive data.

People should change their passwords regularly, perhaps every three months.

Sensitive data should only be accessible by those with authority to view it. Your IT Information Technology administrator should design your systems so that there are secure areas.

Taking data away should be restricted or possibly you may want to have a policy banning it. Policies should also cover the use of USB keys and other external storage devices, as they pose a threat of introducing viruses and can be used to take away copies of data.

Telephone security

Telephones, especially mobile phones, can be a point of information vulnerability. This is especially the case if authorities and police are hostile. But even individuals with the right technology or capabilities can hack into your phone and, for example, access messages. Be careful with your mobile phone, be cautious in leaving and recording messages. The use of code words, and other simple precautions, may make your ministry more secure. At a minimum make sure your mobile phone has a passcode to open it.

Email security

Emails travel through cyberspace and leave traces. Even if you delete them from your own computer there will be copies on the servers of the internet companies through which the message has travelled.

Sensitive information needs to be handled carefully. Emails are a key tool of many ministries and it can be difficult to operate without them. So wisdom in what you write is vital. If operating in a hostile country where the security forces of the authorities are probably scanning the internet, you may need to use a set of simple key code words to talk about you work with your associates. For example "Christian", "converts", "evangelist", "Bibles", "pastor", "worship", "prayer" are key sensitive words in some contexts and your group should perhaps agree to call them "friend", "youngsters", "teacher", "books", "papa", "meeting" and "discussion" – words that will not trigger any flags in official search engines but that are easily understood in the context in which you work. Thus the sentence

"Pastor David will take the Bibles to the next worship and prayer meeting for convert Christians" becomes the much safer:

"Papa David will take the books to the next meeting and discussion session for youngster friends."

A number of organisations already have simple versions of this for communicating among their own staff and with their overseas partners.

Cyber security
The term cyber security refers to policies and practices that you should consider in order to avoid online fraud or theft of data. Each day, globally, the cost of fraud is more than one billion dollars – that is $1,000,000,000.

In most cases, it is weeks before you discover that you have been hacked or defrauded. Most organisations will suffer a security breach in any 12 months. However, it is also the case that most small organisations believe that they are too small to suffer a cyber-attack.

Your people are often your biggest weakness when it comes to cyber security. The cyber attack is carefully designed to lead someone to disclose information or let in spy-ware or a virus.

1. Phishing emails
A phishing email is one that looks as though it comes from a reputable source (someone you know, your bank, a well-known company) but actually comes from a fraudster or hacker.

- These are usually intended to get you to click on a hyperlink or open an attachment. Doing this may introduce software that can spy on your computer, or introduce a bad virus
- Common tactics to scare you into doing this is to say that your account has been blocked and you need to reopen it,

or that your account has been hacked and you need to take some security precautions, or that a payment is overdue and you risk large penalties
- Alternatively they may tempt you with information that you are owed a payment, perhaps a credit for "overpayment" in the past, or have won a prize or money. If you have never bought a lottery ticket, you are not likely to have won a major prize!
- So never click on a link or open an attachment until you have checked the email and made sure that it is genuine/safe
- Were you expecting this email? If you do not recognise the sender it is not necessarily a cause for alarm. You should however look carefully at the name and email address – is it trying to pretend to be someone you know, is it their normal email address?
- What does the subject line say? Is it alarmist, trying to scare you into doing something quickly without caution?
- Is there a logo from a well-known company e.g. Microsoft or a bank? If the logo is of poor quality, it is probably a copy. Is it a real company?
- How are you addressed? An email that starts 'Dear You' or 'Dear John@wellsfargoinc.com' is probably not from someone who knows you or someone with serious business to discuss
- Look out for bad spelling, bad grammar and bad layout. If from a reputable company it would not normally be badly phrased. Much phishing is written in English to reach a broad audience, so words may be odd or sound disjointed
- When considering clicking on a link, first hover your mouse over the link (without clicking) and this will reveal the true link. This may provide a clue that the link is dangerous
- Check the signature on the email – does it look genuine?

2. Vishing attempts
Vishing refers to attempts to speak to you by telephone and get you to reveal confidential information.

- The caller will often pretend to be a police officer, an official at your bank, or someone similar
- They may have some basic information about you that they will use to try to establish their official status, possibly

quoting your address, date of birth or any other information that is relatively easy to obtain
- They will tell you of a problem that is occurring with your bank account, bank card, credit card, or a contract
- They will ask you some "security questions" so that you can prove who you are. These questions may lead to questions asking you to "verify" account numbers, PIN codes or other confidential information. A real bank, police officer, company would never ask for such confidential information
- The fraud may include sending an official courier to pick up cards or other records from you
- In telephone calls of this nature, it is often worth asking them some security questions in return or better still, say that you will call them back at the bank, police station etc.

3. Smishing
Smishing stands for SMS phishing and is similar to phishing except it is done by text message rather than email. As many banks now use text messages this can be quite convincing. However, your bank should never ask you for account information or ask you to confirm/correct account information. If in doubt, contact your bank directly.

4. Malware
Malware is bad software that will attack your computer or your security. In some ways a virus that causes problems with your system is better than hidden viruses which are spying on you.

Malware gives the fraudster or attacker access to information inside the computer: personal information, account numbers, account details, passwords, key logging and mouse movement, and can even relay your screen to someone else.

A Trojan virus may open a backdoor to your system, allowing an attacker remote access to all your files and systems.

Malware can come through removable storage systems e.g. USB keys, embedded in documents and files, through links and downloads, or via an infected network.

5. Passwords

Passwords are often the key to your systems. People try to obtain your passwords by deception (tricking you into revealing it), spyware (recording your log-in), shoulder surfing (watching over your shoulder as you type on the keyboard) or brute force (an automated attempt to guess your password via multiple attempts).

Common passwords, used because they are easy to remember, are "12345678", "09876543", "password", "qwertyui", "welcome", "letmein", "login", "football", "princess", "starwars" etc. If you are using any of these, your system can be cracked in about 2 seconds. You should use a combination of letters, numbers and other characters. Your password should be a minimum of 8 characters long, preferably 10 or 12 characters.

A good password might be "$peter&19A3%". With random characters, an 8-character password would need over 40,000,000,000,000 attempts to crack it. A national security service might be able to manage it, over time, but you would be safe in most other cases.

6. Common types of cyber attack

Man in the Middle attacks are when someone gets into your network and watches transactions between two people, stealing the information that they have seen. This is a particular danger when using public Wi-Fi, as you do not know how the traffic is handled and who might be watching.

Brute Force attacks are multiple attempts to crack your password, normally using an automated system. The attacker tries thousands of combinations in an attempt to get lucky and hit the right one. See the section above about passwords for how to improve the strength of your passwords.

DDOS Distributed Denial of Service attacks are when your system gets thousands of connections/messages at the same time so flooding the victim. This can come from a single source but it often comes from multiple sources which have themselves been infected by a virus to attack other systems.

Invoice Fraud attacks are fictitious claims for payment. This could consist of a request to change the destination of an authentic payment from an authentic supplier to a fraudulent account. It could be a completely fraudulent invented invoice or demand for payment, made by email, fax, phone or possibly letter. Good financial controls are important here (see section 7 on Financial Security).

Trojan attacks are attempts to take control of your computer. You may get a message asking you to update some software. You are prompted to enter a number and PIN to start the new download. Instead a Trojan programme downloads and takes control of your computer and starts to steal money. If this is an open attack at least you know it is happening. Secret Trojans can be worse, because you don't know it is happening and cannot stop the bank account process.

Fake Orders attacks are messages that appear to come from someone in authority but in fact come from a fraudster. The fraudster may send an email that appears to come from the chairman or managing director (because he has hacked into your system). The email gives you instructions to make a payment or take another action. The instructions might be marked "Highly Confidential" so you cannot check with colleagues. The email might come on a Friday afternoon so you don't have much time to check back.

The main Do's and Don'ts – summary

- Never reveal personal or financial data including usernames, passwords, PINs or ID numbers
- Always take care that people and organisations you are dealing with are genuine. A real bank or reputable organisation will never ask for security information over the phone, by email or SMS
- Never open attachments or hyperlinks from unknown sources
- Always have good strong passwords, at the very least 8 characters long and a mix of letters, numbers and symbols

Always change your password or PIN if you think someone has learned it, and anyway regularly change passwords and PINs as a matter of course

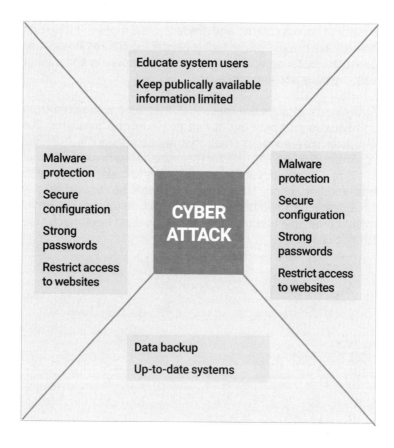

CHAPTER NINE
LEGAL
SECURITY

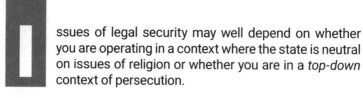

ssues of legal security may well depend on whether you are operating in a context where the state is neutral on issues of religion or whether you are in a *top-down* context of persecution.

Can Christians exist legally in your country? Can Christians meet together freely to pray and worship, to study the Bible, to educate their children, to train their leaders? Can churches be formed, and own property and undertake the normal activities of a fellowship? Can Christian theology colleges or Bible schools operate? Are other activities such as publication of Scriptures and other Christian literature possible? Can Christians operate youth and children's camps, or run schools, clinics or other social activities?

If the answer to all the above questions is "no", for example as in North Korea, then you are essentially in a situation often known as the underground church. The Body of Christ has virtually no public visibility, and the believers have to keep it that way in order to survive. They may draw strength from the fact that this has been a common situation since the times of the Early Church under the Roman Empire, and down the centuries under severe persecution.

However, in this situation there can be no legal security and you may move on to the next chapters.

For those groups operating in contexts of some public recognition, there is the possibility of some legal security. This chapter and the next look at some key issues.

Legal registration

One of the key issues facing many churches, ministries, NGOs and other groups is that of registration of an organisation. Your country may require churches and other Christian groups to be officially registered. In theory this requirement is against human rights law, but it may be a case of necessity to protect your work.

It should be noted that registration is common in many free democratic countries; however, it is not a legal requirement but rather an option you can freely choose, an option that carries many advantages. Advantages may include official recognition, access to state services, a number of financial advantages e.g. state subsidies such as cheaper utility costs, and often tax relief for members' charitable or religious-purpose donations.

In many countries where Christians are under pressure, registration of churches is a requirement which allows the state to limit Christian groups, watch and monitor them, and make unregistered activity illegal. Should this be the case then it is important to make clear that registration requirements are actually contrary to international human rights norms.

In many situations however it may be deemed best to obtain official registration. Apart from becoming a potential shield against official harassment, it also can act as a useful tool when dealing with police, difficult officials and the local administration. It is also useful for public relations, as registration shows that you are in some way "approved" by the authorities as a genuine *bona fide* organisation. This may help deflect criticism from the local population.

It is important to keep registration up to date; this may include filing annual documentation. In some countries the state changes the registration rules quite often, so forcing constant re-registration. Churches, ministries and other groups should keep a watch for such changes. It may be necessary to file audited accounts, and this is another reason why financial security, (chapter 7) is so important.

Ownership of property

Does your church or ministry own land or buildings? How secure is that ownership? Land ownership can be very different in different parts of the world, and in many places land/building ownership is based on tradition and history. However, it is a common tactic for enemies of the faith to try to take away land and buildings from churches and ministries – a very effective way of attacking the Body of Christ.

It is wise to try to protect these assets by registration and other legal methods. If you buy land or buildings, ensure that the ownership is legally registered as robustly as possible. Make sure if possible that ownership is vested in the organisation, not in the name of one or several individual persons. Some donor organisations like Barnabas Fund will refuse to help finance land and building projects if the legal ownership is not securely held by the organisation. It is not that the leader or leaders are not trustworthy, but anything can happen to them and then the ownership of valuable property becomes at risk.

Similar considerations should also be taken for other valuable property: vehicles, computer equipment, stocks of goods etc. For example, if the organisation owns a vehicle or vehicles, they should be registered to the organisation not to the persons who use them.

Other regulations and certification

There are a number of other areas that you may need to check, areas where hostile officials could move against you for non-conformity with the law. This could include building permits, use-of-building registration, health and safety certification, fire regulations etc. You will want to try to stay within the law and regulations on these issues, as failure on sensible rules will be a poor witness to others. You may find that official rules on some issues can be deliberately obstructive, such as the previous Egyptian requirement for a presidential decree for even minor alterations/repair work on a church building. In such cases you may be faced with some difficult choices. Nevertheless if you can stay within the law on these issues it will be both good practice and a protection against official problems.

Legal issues with individuals

There are a number of issues surrounding individuals that should be handled wisely. This includes persons within your organisation. Contracts, employment, salaries, bonuses, pension funds, loans, housing support, expenses incurred or advanced are examples of areas that can lead to difficulties, especially if relationships or situations change.

It can be wise to have clear legal documents setting out relationships, responsibilities and duties – including financial relationships. When employing staff, you may want to have a policies and procedures document outlining general rules for all and have individual employment contracts for each person engaged. This can help avoid conflict and problems both within the organisation and with others. It is often tempting to leave things undefined in the enthusiasm of the moment, but later on it can be problematic when points of view diverge and areas of contention arise. Many readers will know of situations where personal relationships have deteriorated within an organisation or between organisations, and there have been splits on bad terms. These can lead to court cases where there is a dispute over employment terms, bonuses owed, ownership of vehicles or equipment, contracts, bills unpaid etc. This is a bad witness to the Gospel and will be used by enemies to portray the Body of Christ in a bad light.

A contract or legal relationship keeps things neutral and clear, away from personal interpretations, and can help avoid court cases and loss of time and money.

Legal issues across organisations

When contracting with other organisations it is important to be clear and on solid legal ground in the relationship. If you are constructing a building, you need to "lock up" the contract with your architect/engineer/constructor. Construction projects can very easily overrun their budget if they are not strictly controlled and overseen. A construction project running on a week-by-week basis is a recipe for delays and costs overruns, and stress. A good practice can be to include an independent professional project manager or a quantity surveyor, who works for you, to oversee the builder and the sub-contractors, within a solid legal agreement or framework.

Other typical contractual relationships that need good foundations are for the supply of other goods and services such as vehicles, transport services, construction materials, food in large quantities, repair and maintenance services etc.

Professional advice

Do you have access to good professional legal advice, perhaps from someone within the Christian community? It may be a good investment to double-check you legal position on some of these issues and seek advice on how best to improve your resilience.

Working together

It may be a good idea to have networking across Christian groups on these issues, with perhaps an action group including Christian lawyers. This group can advise churches, ministries and others on how to complete the legal process for each requirement, and assist if things become difficult with the authorities.

How active is the Church as a whole on issues of official and legal persecution, discrimination and bias in your country? Is this something that needs to be addressed, perhaps in alliance with other human rights groups in the country? This is addressed more fully in the next chapter.

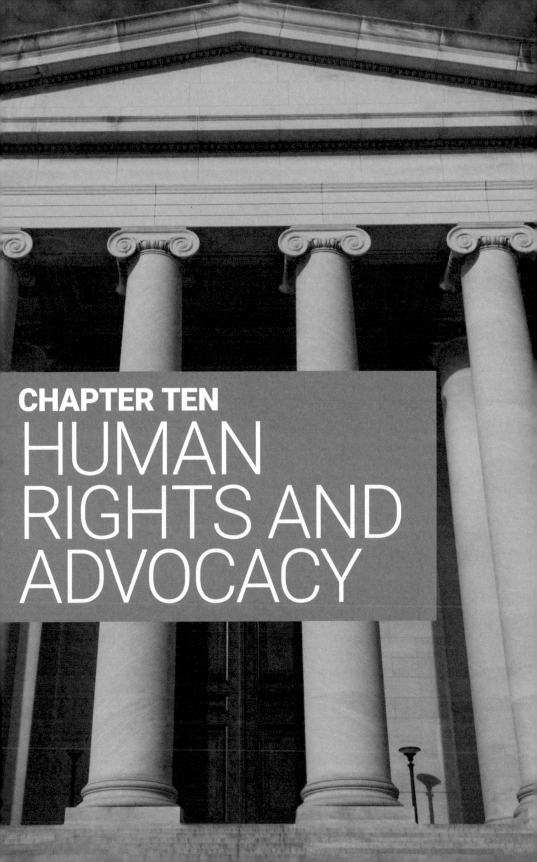

CHAPTER TEN
HUMAN RIGHTS AND ADVOCACY

Human Rights and Religious Freedom

Under international concepts of human rights and religious liberty, there is no requirement for Christians (or anyone else) to be authorised to believe or personally practise their faith. The right to freedom of religious belief, the internal state of belief, is absolute and cannot be legally restricted in any way.

Everyone has the right to freedom of thought, conscience and religion; this right includes freedom to change his religion or belief, and freedom, either alone or in community with others and in public or private, to manifest his religion or belief in teaching, practice, worship and observance.

Article 18, Universal Declaration of Human Rights, 1948

The most quoted and powerful example of this right is Article 18 of the 1948 Universal Declaration of Human Rights. However, it should be noted that this is a "declaration" and is not binding on countries. It does not carry great legal weight but always carries significant moral weight.

However, there are a variety of other instruments that many states have signed up to which are more binding. Possibly the most robust of these instruments is the International Covenant on Civil and Political Rights to which many states have committed themselves since 1976.

<blockquote>

Article 18 of the International Covenant on Civil and Political Rights

1. Everyone shall have the right to freedom of thought, conscience and religion. This right shall include freedom to have or to adopt a religion or belief of his choice, and freedom, either individually or in community with others and in public or private, to manifest his religion or belief in worship, observance, practice and teaching.

2. No one shall be subject to coercion which would impair his freedom to have or to adopt a religion or belief of his choice.

3. Freedom to manifest one's religion or beliefs may be subject only to such limitations as are prescribed by law and are necessary to protect public safety, order, health, or morals or the fundamental rights and freedoms of others.

4. The States Parties to the present Covenant undertake to have respect for the liberty of parents and, when applicable, legal guardians to ensure the religious and moral education of their children in conformity with their own convictions.

</blockquote>

The situation on the right to practise your faith is more complex. In essence freedom is guaranteed to practice your religion, and to gather peacefully with others for purposes of worship, prayer, study, discussion – except for overriding reasons of State for purposes of public safety, order, health, morals, or the protection of rights and freedoms of others. Many states try to use these excuses to legislate restrictive rules against Christians and other minorities, but such actions can be contested in public debate, by advocacy, and by legal action (national and international).

It should be noted that restrictions on religious freedom may not be based on interests of national security. In this there is a difference from the rights of general peaceful assembly protected by Article 21 – and so any attempts to enlarge the scope of limitations to practice of your faith should be strongly resisted.

> **Article 21 of the International Covenant on Civil and Political Rights**
>
> *The right of peaceful assembly shall be recognized. No restrictions may be placed on the exercise of this right other than those imposed in conformity with the law and which are necessary in a democratic society in the interests of national security or public safety, public order (ordre public), the protection of public health or morals or the protection of the rights and freedoms of others.*

It is important that the Church, in its largest sense, maintains vigilance on these issues and remember that restrictions on any part of the Body of Christ can be extended to others.

Strong lobbying and advocacy activity should be considered, especially if your country is bound by elements in its constitution, and its signature on international covenants, declarations, regional agreements or other documents. Public opinion can be a powerful force if you are able to mobilise other supporters, perhaps human rights groups, lawyers, academics, other minorities, parts of the media etc.

In Acts chapter 16, Paul and Silas in Philippi had a typical example of persecution. We read:

> *20 They brought them before the magistrates and said, "These men are Jews, and are throwing our city into an uproar 21 by advocating customs unlawful for us Romans to accept or practice."*
> *22 The crowd joined in the attack against Paul and Silas, and the magistrates ordered them to be stripped and beaten with rods. 23 After they had been severely*

flogged, they were thrown into prison, and the jailer was commanded to guard them carefully. 24 When he received these orders, he put them in the inner cell and fastened their feet in the stocks.

35 When it was daylight, the magistrates sent their officers to the jailer with the order: "Release those men." 36 The jailer told Paul, "The magistrates have ordered that you and Silas be released. Now you can leave. Go in peace."

37 But Paul said to the officers: "They beat us publicly without a trial, even though we are Roman citizens, and threw us into prison. And now do they want to get rid of us quietly? No! Let them come themselves and escort us out."

38 The officers reported this to the magistrates, and when they heard that Paul and Silas were Roman citizens, they were alarmed. 39 They came to appease them and escorted them from the prison, requesting them to leave the city.

It is important that Christians stand up for their rights when these are available in the constitution or the legal system. This is not only to protect your rights but also to protect the rights of brothers and sisters. One of the commonest problems for Christians in many countries is that of the impunity of perpetrators of illegal acts, be they officials, police or members of the majority faith.

Impunity encourages extremists and enemies of Christianity to act against the Church, Christian communities or individuals. They know that nothing will happen to them and they will not be punished. In turn others see this and start to copy persecutory actions. Before long there is a general tendency of groups to act violently and illegally.

It takes courage and commitment to challenge persecution, especially from the authorities, and it may be important to draw in support from other sources. Human rights NGOs, lawyers, the press, political activists and international agencies should all be considered as potential allies for justice.

A modern example could be this May 2016 story from a Christian media source in Pakistan [4]

Four police dismissed after torture of two Christian prisoners

Pakistan People's Party co-chairman Bilawal Bhutto Zardari, has taken the Lahore police to task for inhumanely torturing two Christians. While condemning the police's obnoxious attitude, he demanded that those responsible for the cruelty be expelled and taught a lesson. He clarified that any form of violence against anybody will not be tolerated by PPP.

In keeping with details, two Christians were booked by the investigation wing of the Lahore's Shalimar police over charges of fraud. While carrying out the investigations the police hung one of the men upside down from a bunk and tortured him inhumanely. The other was stripped naked and tortured. While in custody, police subjected 30-year-old Faraz Masih and 40-year-old Doya Masih to brutal forms of torture. Followed by media reports on the incident, police tried to justify the abject investigatory torture by claiming these captives have confessed to more than 12 instances of robbery.

Consequently, the S.P. Investigations took notice of the incident and issued orders of dismissal of Hammad Butt in charge of investigations, ASI Tariq, Constable Sadiq and Arif.

4 http://www.christiansinpakistan.com/bilawal-bhutto-slams-lahore-police-for-savagely-torturing-two-christians/ [viewed 25/5/16]

The dismissals of the violent policemen came about because of media attention, public interest and protest, and then political involvement.

If an incident occurs, it is very important to record the main details accurately. This will help you in your case, will help you with the media, and will help you when generating international attention. It is surprising how vague initial reports of incidents can be and this damages the possibility of getting quick focus on the incident.

- Where did the incident take place?
- When did it happen; date and time?
- Who was involved; the victims?
- Who was involved; the perpetrators?
- What happened?
- Who witnessed this?
- What happened afterwards?
- What complaints have been registered; who with, when?
- What additional details are available; doctors' statements, police reference numbers, police station address?

You should try to register complaints with the authorities if possible. Get a record or police registration number of the complaint.

Try to get assistance as soon as possible, perhaps a specialist organisation, or a Christian lawyer.

Publicise the issue locally, nationally and internationally if it is safe to do so and if this might help your case.

Put your arguments in terms of upholding law and order, justice, equality for all, the country's constitutional protections, human rights, the country's duty under international conventions.

CHAPTER ELEVEN

WORKING WITH OTHERS

 **It** is absolutely essential that your leadership engages with other organisations and individuals that can help you. You may have members of the church who have skills or experience in the field, such as police officers, security workers, or from the military, medics and nurses, lawyers.

A number of services may be there to provide assistance in case of need, such as the police, fire brigade, medical services. Other organisations and individuals will be able to give you advice and other assistance, such as police advisors, and specialists within your fellowship. You may want to include a security element in your review of the fabric of the building, with an eye to making it more resistant to attack e.g. minimising risk of glass shards in the event of an explosion, resistance to arson, security of information.

Local services

- In any disaster-type event, you need to know who and where are your local services, especially emergency services
- Contact details must be up to date, readily available and distributed
- Meet with professionals and discuss; get advice
- Implement any recommendations they make to you
- Meet them on a regular basis e.g. annually

Liaison with police and specialised officers

- Make personal contact with your local police force, if appropriate
- Local police station, contact telephone number? Dedicated officer with whom you liaise?
- Maintain good contacts, don't let them lapse

Liaison with fire brigade

- Make personal contact with your local fire brigade, if appropriate
- Obtain fire brigade advice, guidance and help with risk assessments, measures to take or training
- Maintain good contacts, don't let them lapse

Liaison with medical services

You may want to investigate local medical services, and the types of assistance available in different places. For example, where is the best local hospital, or accident and emergency department? Where is the nearest specialist burns unit? Also, what capabilities do you have within the fellowship, in terms of first-aiders, paramedics, nurses, doctors and other medical practitioners?

You will probably want to:
- Know what and where are your local emergency services
- Have details up to date, readily available and distributed
- Have designated trained first-aiders (generally good practice anyway)
- Have basic first aid kits available on site and easy to find

Community relations

- Work at establishing and maintaining a good relationship with the local community and individual communities
- A church which has strong links to the local community may gain some security benefits – the local public may "keep an eye" on the church and be more favourable to its activities
- Work to promote community cohesion
- Establish, if possible, a visibly good working relationship with the local religious leaders of other faiths (and also other Christian denomination leaders). Work together on useful community initiatives. This may pay many dividends in harmonious community relations, and good public relations, not to mention opportunities for Christian witness
- However, do be very cautious about interfaith initiatives, if they could compromise the Christian faith

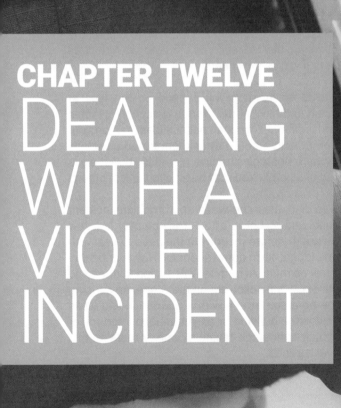

CHAPTER TWELVE
DEALING WITH A VIOLENT INCIDENT

If, despite all your measures to prevent an incident, there does occur an attack on your church or ministry, then the initial response will be critical. How you respond in the first few minutes or hours will make a big difference to the impact, to the survivors, to the viability of your church/ministry and its reputation.

You may want to rehearse and practice plans and scenarios, very much as you may carry out fire drills to test alarms and procedures. Everyone must know what to do, where to go, how to respond. The more you are trained the easier a response will be during the chaos of an event.

The first priority should be people, whether it is to evacuate the site, tend to the injured or ensure that no further injuries are sustained. Almost in parallel you must ensure that the emergency services are alerted, and you are ready to render as much assistance to them as they need.

How you respond to an incident will depend on the type of incident, and you should have some standard scenarios within your thinking and planning. Typical possibilities to consider might be an arson attack, a bomb attack, an armed attack by one or more persons, a hostage situation, a credible threat e.g. a telephone warning of a bomb. You may be able to think of others.

It may be useful to distinguish between an immediate incident and an ongoing incident. A bomb attack may be over in a few seconds, and you are therefore faced with the need to deal with the immediate and longer-term consequences. However bear in mind that there may be multiple bombs with a second due to go off at a later stage e.g. when police are on the scene. An ongoing incident would be an arson attack with a fire continuing while people are still inside the building or as yet unaccounted for, or else an armed attack or hostage-taking by one or more people that continues over a period.

Ongoing incidents
Planning might include consideration of courses of action where staff can most effectively respond to an armed attack situation, so as to minimise loss of life/injury. Thinking through options

for response can save valuable time, as depicting scenarios and considering response options in advance will assist individuals and groups to quickly select their best course of action.

This is a very sensitive topic. You may well decide that only leaders, staff and stewards should be sensitised to these issues, and the fellowship in general should not be alarmed at this point. If later you feel that the level of threat has risen from "very unlikely" to "possible", especially if it is a topic of public concern among your members, you may then decide to have an open conversation with the whole fellowship. Though some people may find the conversation uncomfortable, they may also find it reassuring to know that as a whole their church is thinking ahead about how best to deal with any situation.

During an active terrorist attack, the natural human reaction is to be startled, to feel fear and anxiety and even to experience initial disbelief and denial. Noise from alarms, gunfire, explosions, and people shouting and screaming should be expected. Advance planning and perhaps training provides key personnel with the means to regain composure, recall at least some of what has been learned, and take action.

Respond immediately

It is common for people confronted with a threat to first deny the possible danger rather than respond. Some people might insist they are hearing firecrackers, when in fact they hear gunfire. Train key personnel to skip denial and to respond immediately.

For example, train people to recognise the sounds of danger, act, and forcefully communicate the danger and necessary action (e.g., "Gun! Get out!"). In addition, those closest to a communications system should communicate the danger and necessary action to others. Repetition in training and preparedness shortens the time it takes to orient, observe, and act. Upon recognising the danger, as soon as it is safe to do so, staff or others should alert first responders by contacting the emergency services with as clear and accurate information as possible.

There are three basic response options: run, hide, or fight. Individuals can run away from the gunman; seek a secure place where they can hide and/or deny the terrorist access; or incapacitate the terrorist(s) in order to survive and protect others from harm.

As the situation develops, it is possible that staff and others will need to use more than one option. During an active situation, these individuals will rarely have all of the information they need to make a fully informed decision about which option is best. While they should follow the plan and any instructions given during an incident, they will often have to rely on their own judgment to decide which option will best protect lives, their own and others.

Run

If it is safe to do so, the first course of action that should be taken is to evacuate the building and move far away until in a safe location. People should be trained, as for a fire evacuation, to:

- Leave personal belongings behind
- Visualize possible escape routes, including physically accessible routes for individuals with disabilities
- Avoid escalators and lifts
- Go to a safe meeting point where people can be counted and checked
- Take others with them, assisting people who are less mobile
- Call security services when safe to do so
- If there are children, to let a responsible adult know where they are

Hide

If running is not a safe option, hide in as safe a place as possible. Key people should be trained to assist others to hide in a location where the walls might be thicker and have fewer windows. In addition:

- Lock the doors
- Barricade the doors with heavy furniture
- Close and lock windows and close blinds or cover windows
- Turn off lights
- Silence all electronic devices
- Remain silent
- If possible, use strategies to silently communicate with first responders; for example, in rooms with exterior windows, make signs to silently signal police and emergency responders to indicate the status of the room's occupants
- Hide along the wall closest to the exit but out of the view from the hallway (allowing for an ambush of a gunman and for possible escape if a terrorist enters the room)
- Remain in place until given an all-clear by identifiable law enforcement
- If items are falling from above – get under a sturdy table
- If you're trapped in debris, stay close to a wall and tap on pipes so that rescuers can hear you
- Don't use matches or lighters in case of gas leaks

Fight

If neither running nor hiding is a safe option, as a last resort, when confronted by a terrorist, adults in immediate danger should consider trying to disrupt or incapacitate him/her by using aggressive force and items in their environment, such as fire extinguishers or chairs. In an American study[5] of 41 active 'shooter events' that ended before law enforcement arrived, the potential victims themselves stopped the attacker in 16 instances. In 13 of those cases, they physically subdued the attacker.

---

5 Blair, J Peter and M Hunter Martaindale, United States Active Shooter Events from 2000 to 2010: Training and Equipment Implications, Texas State University, [n.d.], http://tinyurl.com/zgurg6k [viewed 13/3/2016]

While talking to the staff and possibly the congregation about confronting an armed attacker may be daunting and upsetting for some, they should know that they might be able to successfully take action to save lives. How each individual chooses to respond if directly confronted is up to him or her.

Interacting with emergency services

If a shooting or armed attack occurs, staff and key personnel should be trained to understand and expect that police and security forces' first priority must be to locate and stop the person or persons believed to be the attackers; all other actions are secondary. Staff should be trained to cooperate and not to interfere with first responders. They should understand that police are operating with little information, and do not know who are staff and church/ministry members—everyone is a potential terrorist/accomplice until proven otherwise. So display empty hands with open palms, obey instructions, and anticipate that police may tell everyone to place their hands on their heads or lie on the ground.

In an ongoing terrorist situation, police may find it useful to receive information about the building, perhaps a site plan, access to CCTV systems, or anything else that may help them swiftly master the situation with minimum loss of life. These items should be easily accessible and staff should know where they are located.

Immediately after an incident

Once the initial attack incident is over, emergency services will work with church staff and victims on a variety of matters. This will include securing the site, tending the injured, interviewing witnesses, gathering evidence and initiating an investigation.

Police and others may require plans of the site, information about alarm systems, CCTV, gas mains, identification of witnesses, names and addresses.

The church/ministry should identify trained personnel who will provide assistance to victims and their families. This should include assisting those physically injured, comforting those traumatised, supporting families and assisting the leadership in dealing with the aftermath. This team will need to liaise with local services. One important area would be having good information about everyone hurt in an incident, and where they have been taken for treatment. Parents of children, for example, will be desperate to know if their son or daughter is safe, and which hospital they have gone to if injured.

Where the immediate reunification of loved ones is not possible, providing family members with timely, accurate, and relevant information is paramount. Having family members wait for long periods for information about their loved ones not only adds to their stress and frustration, but can also escalate the emotions of the entire group. How you handle this area may be crucial for the fellowship, its public reputation and its private duty of love and care.

When families are reunited, it is critical that there are good child release processes in place where minors might be involved (e.g. Sunday school, youth group, childcare, religious education classes) to assure that no child is released to an unauthorised person, even if that person is well meaning. This would normally be part of your child protection policy.

Essential steps to help establish trust and provide family members with a sense of control can be accomplished by:

- Identifying a safe location in which to wait, separate from distractions and/or media and the general public, but close enough to allow family members to feel connected in proximity to their children/loved ones
- Scheduling periodic updates even if no significant additional information is available
- Providing some basic refreshments
- Being prepared to speak with family members about what to expect when reunified with their child/loved ones
- Ensuring effective communication with those that have language barriers or need other accommodations, such as sign language interpreters for the hearing impaired

Media

Within its planning, the church/ministry should explicitly address how it will engage with media attention, and how affected families will be supported if they prefer not to engage with the media. This includes strategies for keeping the media separate from families if the emergency is ongoing (e.g. a hostage situation) and support for families who may experience unwanted media attention at their homes.

The church may be able to access professional media relations experts via its denomination, and this could be part of the advance planning research.

A strong Christian statement after a major incident can have wide coverage and be a huge witness for the Gospel. You may well know of remarkable testimonies after terror outrages.[6]

It is difficult to plan too much in advance, but at least thinking through possibilities and knowing who will be the media spokesperson will prepare you significantly.

---

6 www.mirror.co.uk/news/uk-news/james-foleys-parents-prepared-forgive-4092566 and http://lancasterpa.com/amish/amish-forgiveness [both viewed 15/8/2016]

It is important to take charge of the narrative in a news story. You want your story told, not a story from anyone hostile or a story made up by the media to provide sensational news. You may find that you are only providing one version of the story, but yours needs to be told.

Without being overtly critical of media and journalists, it must be said that many inexperienced people have bad experiences with the media and come away afterwards bruised and saddened that the story is unrecognisable and they have been portrayed in a totally erroneous manner. The media have their own agenda, journalists or their employers may be hostile to Christianity, they have urgent deadlines and can be ruthless getting a dramatic angle that sounds exciting.

Alternatively you may want to say nothing. This is frustrating, but it is sometimes wiser than saying something that you regret later.

However, in most cases the media will be anxious to talk to you and you will be asked for the church's or ministry's reaction to the incident. It might be wise to think about this in advance, even if it is just five minutes' reflection, rather than a hasty sound-bite when you are under pressure.

Think about two or three points you want to make and stick to them. You have probably seen politicians ignoring journalists' questions and just making the statements they want to make – do the same.

- Emphasise the community of the church, its lawful behaviour, local character, community activities, charity work etc.
- Emphasise the impact of the incident, casualties and damage, the suffering of innocent individuals especially children
- Be critical of what people have done e.g. a terrorist attack, but do not leap to conclusions as to why they have done it or make unfounded allegations against any group or individuals, unless someone has claimed responsibility and the case is proven

Use the personal angle of someone in the middle of the incident; it was your church or fellowship attacked, you know the people impacted, give the human dimension and portray the everyday community of your fellowship.

Clearly and calmly refute any false arguments or accusations e.g. that you have provoked the attack by your activities or statements, of being anti-Muslim/Hindu/Buddhist, that you are a cult or Christian extremists/fundamentalists. Emphasise the rights of citizens and human rights.

Explain any controversial issues clearly, but without being either defensive or aggressive. A smile and a gentle answer will go a long way towards disarming critical viewers of a difficult interview. An aggressive interviewer and a calm response by you will win many supporters. If pushed into a corner, you could consider saying that this is a tricky issue and you need to think about it further – not an answer a politician would give, but it may come over as very honest and refreshing! Viewers, listeners or readers will not expect a polished performance from you (a member of the public rather than a professional), but they will expect a church leader or spokesperson to be frank and honest.

As stated earlier, your denomination or network or friends may provide some professional media support. You may want to liaise closely with any spokesperson, so that they do not say anything you find unhelpful – after all they don't know the local context even if they are a great media handler.

Finally don't be too afraid of the media. If you can tell your story in a clear way you may be able to draw on a lot of support from the area and some good may also come out of a bad situation. This may be an opportunity to reach a wide audience and project a simple Christian message of compassion, forgiveness and salvation to people who never otherwise listen to a Christian leader.

The following is a summary of advice useful in many contexts

The nature of any attack will influence the best options for safety; a bomb blast at an occupied building is different from an arson attack on a largely unoccupied building which is different from intruders with guns which is different from a drive-by shooting. Also it is extremely unlikely you will be caught up in a terrorist attack anywhere; however, if you are, try to do the following:

Run

- Escape if you can. Put distance between yourself and the danger
- Consider the safest options
- Is there a safe route? RUN if possible
- Can you get there without exposing yourself to greater danger?
- Insist others leave with you
- Leave belongings behind

Hide

- If you can't run, then HIDE
- Find cover from gunfire e.g. substantial brickwork/heavy reinforced walls
- If you can see the attacker, they may be able to see you
- Cover from view does not always mean you are safe; bullets can go through glass, brick, wood and metal
- Be aware of your exits
- Try not to get trapped
- Be quiet, silence your phone
- Lock/barricade yourself in
- Move away from the door

Tell

- Call the police
- Location – where are the suspects?
- Direction – where did you last see the suspects?
- Descriptions – describe the attacker, numbers, features, clothing and weapons
- Further information – casualties, type of injury, building information, entrances, exits, any hostages
- Stop other people entering the building if it is safe to do so
- Protecting yourself, your staff, your organisation and your community

When armed response officers arrive on the scene, professional advice is the following:

- Follow officers' instructions
- Remain calm
- Can you move to a safer area?
- Avoid sudden movements that may be considered a threat
- Keep your hands in view (i.e. put them in the air or on your head)

Be aware that police or military may:

- Point guns at you
- Treat you firmly
- Question you
- Be unable to distinguish you from the attacker
- Evacuate you when it is safe to do so

> *"We know that **all things** work together for good for those who love God, who are called according to his purpose"*
>
> **Romans 8:28 (emphasis added)**

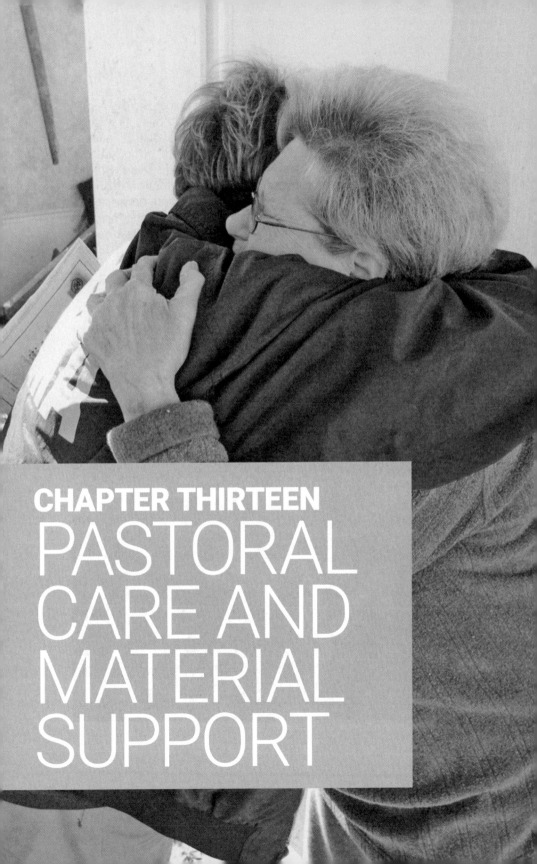

CHAPTER THIRTEEN

PASTORAL CARE AND MATERIAL SUPPORT

A church will have a major role in counselling people about death and injury of loved ones, or missing persons. You probably have trained pastors and people who care for others, or counsellors, and these should be available to assist family members. After an incident, it is critical to confirm that each family is getting the support it needs, from both professionals and the church family, including long-term support. Failure of support in times of difficulty is one of the strongest causes of criticism of some churches. This is a responsibility for the leadership and also the membership. It is critical that families and loved ones are supported as they both grieve any loss and support their surviving family members.

After a major incident, the church/ministry might consider helping with medical costs or family living expenses. For poorer Christians medical costs can be a heavy burden. With serious injuries the costs might be significant for longer-term care. A family may have lost a husband/father and breadwinner, and so they do not even have the normal income that covers food, house rental costs, clothes and other necessities.

As well as pastoral/spiritual support, affected families may need trauma counselling or psychological assistance from trained

professionals. Usually a church cannot provide this, but it should ask victims and assist towards this provision.

People may need some material support. They may have lost their home, their livestock or their possessions. Their loss could be financial, if for example someone is out of work because they are injured or traumatised.

The assistance could be time and energy. It could be help with farming, shopping, or household chores. It could be help with childcare. Some churches have men's groups that are active in the community with practical work. Are these areas where a family could use assistance while recovering?

A good fellowship will think about these things and be proactive in providing help, and maintain this help for as long as it is needed. If the fellowship does not have the resources to help, they could approach leaders within their denomination or network for assistance, or seek help from an outside donor.

In the aftermath of an incident, leaders may need to ensure that they situation is not inflamed by people who want to go after those who attacked them or to stage a retribution attack against another community. Pastors may want to speak about Christian forgiveness, the Church's experience of persecution and martyrdom. The New Testament lesson is that Christians live under the authorities, who are second only to God's authority. Christians should try to stay calm and respect the rule of law.

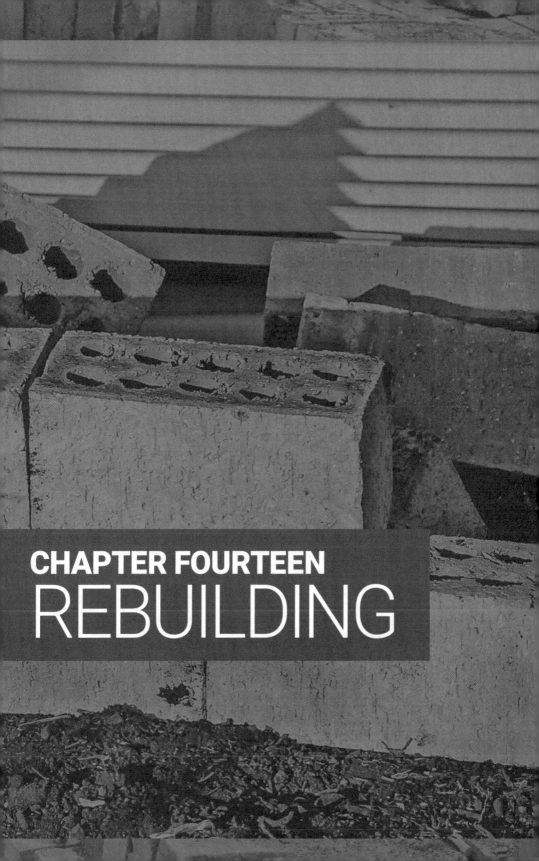

CHAPTER FOURTEEN
REBUILDING

**Y**our church or ministry could face the task of rebuilding after a major incident, whether this is because of loss of a site, building, equipment, data or personnel.

The risk analysis, thinking and the planning that you have done previously should have mitigated the effects of the incident and should have put you in a better place for rebuilding or re-establishing your work.

You will have to cover the material costs of rebuilding or acquiring equipment and materials, but you may be able to secure some assistance in this. You should have safeguarded data and other master documents/materials so that you can quickly reproduce, reprint and restart. You should have a recovery team in place with set tasks for rebuilding. You could have staff, volunteers and church members ready and briefed to help with the task ahead. You could have a fellowship that is confident in a leadership that has planned ahead and is ready to lead the rebuilding.

In previous studies up to 50% of organisations impacted by terrorist bombing went out of business never to return. It is clear that how quickly – and painlessly – you manage to get back to "business as usual" in the event of a terrorist attack, fire, flood

or a natural disaster, or any other major interruption, depends on how effectively you can devise, and put into action, your own organisation continuity plan.

It is important that your church or ministry council, board or senior management is closely involved with the planning, and remains involved in the execution of the recovery plan. People, perhaps a small effective group, from the governing body and senior management need to have ownership of the continuity plan and need to champion it. However, it will be necessary to have everyone on board and to consult with the fellowship regularly to maintain communication and their confidence in progress. You will also want to draw in new skills, help and support as the plan rolls out.

- You need the fullest possible picture of the complex interactions inside your organisation and between activities, leadership, your staff, your members and other people
- You will want to continually help your colleagues and members understand why and how you are dealing with issues and challenges
- You want the fellowship involved and knowing that their contribution is part of the implementation process
- You can include expert knowledge about every part of the organisation within your continuity plan
- You can find out if anyone in the organisation already has experience of plans or procedures to deal with a major incident or terrorist attack

Different departments

During recovery you may need to prioritise certain ministries and "departments". How immediately essential is this work to the church or ministry or the people you are serving? You will need to be objective on this; it is about practicalities not profile. What equipment, IT and other systems does the department need to be able to function? Who else inside or outside the church does the department need to be able to carry out their work? Who else in the church depends on this function?

Sites and facilities

During recovery, if your site is lost or damaged, from where are you going to operate? If your organisation has more than one site, you will need to juggle the possibility of moving some activities to the undamaged site. If you only have one site, you will need to start operating from your back-up site as soon as possible. Your original planning may have contained some suggestions, or you may already have a "what-if" agreement with another church, a hall, a school or similar, to use their site if you lose yours. And are you ready to help another local church or ministry if they have a problem?

Rebuilding plan

You may like to create a chart that shows the various things to do, who is responsible and the time frame for each element. Some things are higher priority, some things will take longer, some things are dependent on others being done first, and some things have important deadlines.

One possibility would be to use a Gantt chart (hypothetical sample on P68. These are commonly used in project management, and are useful ways of showing activities, tasks or events – displayed against time.

On the left of the **chart** is a list of the activities and along the top is a suitable time scale. The activities are clearly shown, with a start date and a projected end date, and the person(s) responsible or in charge are shown within the coloured boxes.

Budgeting is also important, whether this is in liaison with your membership, parent organisation or partners. Budgets should be established for the various tasks and groups, and these should be regularly reviewed by the leadership.

We hope and pray that under the Lord's protection you will never experience attack or need to rebuild your church / ministry activities. However, we also hope that this set of guidance notes will have proved useful in planning for good security and, if the worst should happen, in helping you make a rapid recovery.

May the Lord bless your work in His service.

Dr Patrick Sookhdeo

A sample Gantt chart showing elements in a hypothetical loss of premises for 3–4 months after a terrorist incident.

L = Church leadership P = Pastor(s)

TASK OR ACTIVITY	Wk1	Wk2	Wk3	Wk4	Wk5	Wk6	Wk7	Wk8	Wk9	W10	W11	W12	W13	W14	W15	W16
Set up task groups	L															
Budget control and review	L		L		L		L				L		L		L	
Make arrangements for use of another site	L	L														
Media handling	Person designated by leadership															
Set up temporary church office	Administrator															
Move equipment and material		Men's group														
IT systems re-established		IT team														
Publicise new meeting arrangements			Church Secretary													
Church services in new premises			Leadership and Ministry team													
Pastoral care reviews			P				P				P				P	
New church office operational					Administrator and Church Secretary											
Children's groups operational						Leadership and Children's leaders										
Youth groups operational							Leadership and Youth leaders									
Other activities restart							Leadership and activity leaders									
Review progress and activities; replan									Leadership					Leadership		
Start moving back to own site																
Own site fully operational																

Global Jihad

The Future in the Face of Militant Islam

Patrick Sookhdeo

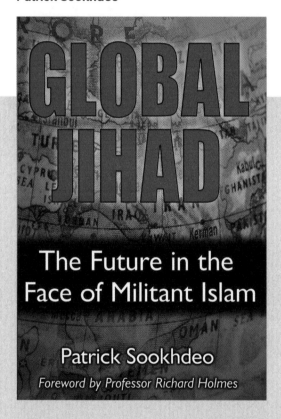

What is the driving force behind Islamic terrorism. Dr. P. Sookhdeo takes an in-depth look at the teachings of Islam past and present, drawing on a wide range of sources including many Muslim writers. He examines aspects of Islam which could motivate violence in its followers. This is an invaluable resource for decision-makers in politics, security, intelligence and the military but will also be of great interest to any reader who seeks to understand Islamic violence in the world today.

Format: Hardback ISBN: 9780978714123 Number of Pages: 669

Unmasking Islamic State

Revealing their motivation, theology and end time predictions

Patrick Sookhdeo

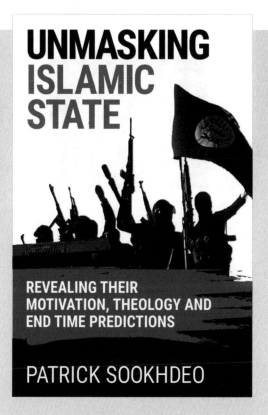

The modern world struggles to make sense of the savage violence and terror perpetrated by Islamic State. In this timely publication Dr Patrick Sookhdeo analyses its ideology, theology, eschatology and strategy and scrutinizes key IS publications explaining the motivating beliefs of the leadership. He exposes the cruel nature of life under IS rule. He argues that it cannot be defeated by military means but must be delegitimised by the encouragement of reform movements within the Muslim community.

Format: Hardback ISBN: 9780996724500 Number of Pages: 200

Fighting the Ideological War

Winning Strategies from Communism to Islamism

Katharine C. Gorka & Patrick Sookhdeo

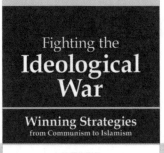

Islamism is a growing and powerful ideology that tolerates no dissent or rivalry. Yet in recent decades the United States has responded only to the violence that Islamism has generated, not to the beliefs and ideas that drive it.

Format: Paperback
ISBN: 9780985310905
Number of Pages: 240

Meeting the Ideological Challenge of Islamism

How to Combat Modern Radical Islam

Anna Bekele & Patrick Sookhdeo

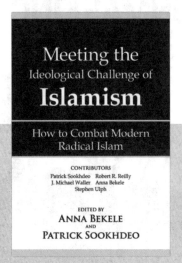

Islamist extremism is one of the most vital issues facing governments and populations today, as Islamist groups turn more violent, with increasing radicalized recruits.

Format: Paperback
ISBN: 978-0-9916145-9-2
Number of Pages: 192